am.

This menu-reader is a handy dictionary of French words and terms connected with food found in restaurants throughout France. Its size is meant to fit in a pocket or handbag and be a quick reference book at the restaurant table.

The book is split into three sections French-English, English-French, and a separate section on French Cheeses, as these are so rarely listed on a menu. Its principles are quite simple:-

> a) items are arranged in strict alphabetical order

> b) there are no capital letters for proper nouns - e.g. saint honoré

> c) on every occasion the prefixes - á la and en is ignored e.g. to find á la mode look up mode (á la), to find en robe, look up robe (en)

> d) as there are so many sauces in French cuisine, they are listed individually and not under sauces - e.g. sauce parisienne can be found by looking under parisienne

> e) the non-French speaker can point to the particular phrase or dish required

Since there are at least 250 ways to cook a fillet of sole, I hope you can appreciate that no work of this size could ever be considered complete. Emphasis has been placed on the food content with only a rudimentary coverage of wines and spirits.

I hope this book helps you to enjoy French food even more, perhaps by trying something different or just by understanding a little better what you are b

Bon Appetit

Maggie Plunkett
Stanway Publications
West Linden Lodge
Colwall, Malvern, Worcs.

July 1999

First Published in UK 1998
This edition published in 1999
by Stanway Publications

Copyright © Maggie Plunkett
Stanway Publications

ISBN 09532 85804

With thanks to

Jeremy, Fiona and Mary

for their encouragement and support

A

abadèche rouge	type of sea bass
abats	offal
abbatis	giblets (fowl)
abignades/abegnades	goose tripe and blood served on fried bread with lemon
abricot	apricot
abricot à la diable	poached glazed apricot on macaroons
abricotine	apricot and brandy liqueur
absinthe	aromatic plant (wormwood) used to flavour vermouth
abusseau	type of sea smelt
accompagnement	garnish/vegetable (served with meat)
acidulés	sharp (acidic)
affiné	ripe
africaine (à l')	dish usually cooked with mushroom, aubergine, tomato and a potato garnish
agenaise (à l')	(oeufs à l')......fried eggs with onions and aubergines
agneau	lamb
agrumes	citrus fruits
aigle de mer	skate
aiglefin	haddock
aïgo à la ménagère	soup of onion, leek, garlic and tomato with poached eggs
aïgo bouïdo	garlic soup - a provençal speciality
aïgo saou	fish and vegetable soup
aigre	sour
aigre doux/douce	bitter sweet
aigrefin	haddock
aigrelet (ette)	sourish tart
aigrette	sour/tart
aigrettes	sourish tart in choux pastry
aiguillette	top rump (beef)
ailes de raie	skate wings
ailier	wing (bird/fish)
aillada	spicy garlic and oil sauce
aillade	garlic and walnut sauce
aillé(e)	garlic-flavoured

aïoli	garlic mayonnaise
aïoli à la grecque	a vinaigrette of garlic and nuts, served with fish
aïoli de morue	salt cod, garlic mayonnaise and vegetables
airelle	cranberry/bilberry
albert	a creamy horseradish sauce
albertine	a sauce based on white-wine, mushrooms and truffles
albuféra (à la d')	poached chicken dish, stuffed with rice, truffles, and foie gras
algérienne	a dish with tomato sauce, red peppers/sweet potato croquettes and tomatoes as main ingredients
algue	seaweed
algue (rouge)	type of seaweed
aligot	potato and cheese purée
aligot au pain	bread and cheese purée
aligoté	type of grape
alise/alisier	service berry (similar to rowan)
allemande	a velouté sauce with mushrooms, also known as "sauce parisienne"
allumette	small strips of puff pastry, sweet or savoury
allumettes	matchstick thickness and length (vegetables)
alose	shad (fish)
alouette	lark
aloyau	sirloin (of beef)
alsacienne (à l')	a dish with ham, sausage and sauerkraut as main ingredients
alsatian	light dry white wine
amande	almond
amandes de mer	small shellfish (dog-cockle)
amandes effilées	flaked almonds
amandes entières	whole almonds
amandes grillées	roasted almonds
amandes hachées	chopped almonds
amandes mondées	blanched almonds
améléon	type of cider
amenlous	almonds baked in pastry
amer	bitter
américaine	garlic, shallots, tomatoes, white wine, brandy lobster or shrimp flavouring

amoricaine	a cultivated oyster
amuse-gueule	cocktail snack
anacarde	cashew nut
ananas	pineapple
anchoïade	an anchovy paste with olive oil, spread on toast or celery
anchois	anchovy
ancienne (l')	dish cooked using traditional methods
andalou (à l')	dish served with tomatoes
andalouse (à l')	with tomatoes, perhaps with rice/sweet peppers
andouille	chiterlings
andouille(tte)	i) grilled/fried seasoned aromatic sausage made from tripe
	ii) small pork sausage
ane	donkey
aneth	dill
ange de mer	angel fish - similar to monkfish
angélique	angelica
anges à cheval	"angels on horseback" oysters wrapped in bacon and fried or grilled
anglaise (à l')	english-style method of cooking.usually plain roasted or boiled
anglois	plum tart
anguille	eel
anis	anise
anis étoilé	star anise
anone	custard apple - (fritters or poached)
antillaise (à l')	dish cooked with rum
aquavit	a potent, colourless scandanavian liqueur - often flavoured with caraway seeds
arachide	peanut/groundnut
araignée (de mer)	spider crab
arapèdes	limpets
archiduc (à l')	a dish with paprika and cream
ardennaise (à l')	a dish with juniper berries
arête (sur l')	fishbone (cooked on the bone)
arête (à l')	on the bone (fish)
argile cuite	terracotta, earthenware
ariégeoise (à l')	dish with cabbage, salt pork and potatoes
arlésienne (à l')	dish with tomatoes, onions, aubergines, potatoes rice or olives
armagnac	brandy

armottes	cornmeal cakes
artésienne (à l')	dish cooked with beer
artichaut	artichoke
artichaut d'hiver	jerusalem artichoke
artichaut du canada	jerusalem artichoke
asperges	asparagus
assaisonnement	dressing/seasoning
assiette(de)	a plateful of ...
assiette anglaise	assorted cold cuts of various meats
assiette de charcuterie	assorted pork products
assiette nordique	smoked fish platter
attente: 30 min	waiting time: 30 minutes
attereau	(metal) skewered food, usually deep fried
attereaux	a skewer of thin slices of vegetables etc. cooked in sauce and deep fried
au	garlic
au bleu	fish freshly poached in a simmering bouillon (stock)
au citron	with lemon
au four	baked
au gratin	dish grilled/baked with crisp brown crust (usually breadcrumbs or grated cheese)
au lait	with milk
aubergines	aubergines (egg plant USA)
aulx	garlic
aumônière	"purse"/wrapping - e.g. pancake
aurore	a velouté sauce of thick tomato purée
avec des glaçons	on the rocks
avocat	avocado
avoine	oatmeal/oats

B

baba	a very light yeast cake
badiane	star anise
bagna caouda	anchovy and butter sauce
baguette	long thin loaf of french bread
baguette de tambour	variety of wild mushroom
baies roses	pink berries

baiser	two small meringues joined with cream
bajoue	pig's cheek
ballotine de volaille	boned, stuffed chicken
ballotines d'agneau	balls of minced lamb and onions coated in eggs/flour and fried
banadry	banana liqueur
banane	banana
bar	bass/sea bass
baraquille	triangular stuffed pastry
barbadine	passion fruit
barbarin	red mullet
barbeau	barbel (fish)
barbecue	barbecued
barbe-de-capucin	wild chicory
barbet	red mullet
barbillon	small barbel (fish)
barbouillade	purée of aubergine/egg plant with cream
barbue	brill
bardatte nantaise	cabbage stuffed with rabbit
bardé	lard/bacon covering braising meat, poultry, or game
barigoule	mushroom
baron	large joint comprising of two legs and a saddle (usually mutton/lamb)
barquettes	small boat-shaped shortcrust pastry cases, garnished with fruit
bartavelle	rock partridge
basilic	basil
bâtarole	thick butter sauce/vienna roll
baudroie-angler	angler fish/monk fish
baudroie lotte	burbot (fish)
baudroie lotte-de-mer	monkfish
bavette	undercut of sirloin
baveuse	runny, moist texture
bayonnaise	a mayonnaise with red peppers, onion and cayenne pepper
béarnaise	creamy slightly piquant sauce, with egg yolks, shallots, vinegar, wine, and peppercorns (tarragon and parsley may be added)
béatrice	a light mayonnaise with extra mustard and lemon juice added

bécasse	woodcock
bécassine	snipe
béchamel	basic white sauce
beignet	fritter/doughnut
beignet - soufflé	warm doughnut
beignets d'animelle	lamb's testicles, cooked as sweetbreads
belon	oyster
bercy	fish stock and white wine velouté sauce (parsley may be added)
bercy (à la)	butter mixed with cooked onions and wine sauce - usually served with entrecôte steak
bergamote	type of orange
bergère (à la)	meat/poultry baked with ham, onions, mushrooms and straw potatoes
bernard l'hermite	hermit crab
bessigne	puff-ball mushrooms
bette	swiss chard
betterave	beet (root)
beurre	butter
beurre blanc	sauce consisting of butter, shallots, vinegar, white wine, crème fraîche or double cream
beurre breton	herb butter
beurre de provence	alioli (garlic sauce)
beurre en pommade	creamed butter
beurre fermier	dairy butter
beurre maître d'hôtel	parsley butter
beurre monté citronné	lemon butter
beurre noir	sauce with browned butter, vinegar and/or lemon juice
beurre vert	herb and butter sauce
bézuque	sea bream
biche	hind or doe
bien cuit	well done (cooked meat)
bière	beer
bière brune	mild ale
bifteck	beef steak (fillet)
bigarade	bitter orange sauce
bigorneau(x)	winkle (s)
biguénée	slice of ham between two pancakes
biscotte	melba toast
biscuits	biscuits

biscuits d'anchois a la royale	salty, savoury biscuits topped with anchovy cream
biscuits salés	crackers
bisque	seafood chowder/soup
bisquebouille	a creamy fish soup with anis and garlic
bisque d'écrevisses	crayfish chowder/soup
bisque de homard	lobster chowder/soup
bistorto	brioche ring with saffron and anise
blade	type of sea bream
blanc - cassis	chilled white wine mixed with a blackcurrant syrup (apéritif)
blanc (de poularde)	white meat (breast of chicken)
blanc d'oeuf	egg white
blanc manger	blancmange
blanchaille	whitebait
blanchet	small clam
blanquette	a stew usually of veal, lamb, fowl or seafood with a white sauce
bléa tourte	vegetable tart with pine-nuts and currants
blé noir	buckwheat flour
blette	swiss chard
bleu (à)	cooked very rare (normally steak)
bleu (au)	used to describe fish boiled in salted water, seasoned with vegetables, herbs and wine
blonde/brune	light/dark
blondir	to cook gently in hot fat until pale gold in colour
body	a terrine of veal and bacon
boeuf à la mode	beef simmered in red wine with vegetables and herbs (can be served as clear soup)
boeuf bourguignon	rich beef stew braised in red burgandy wine with vegetables
bois (au) de chêne	food smoked over oak wood
bois boudran	vinegar sharpened salsa of shallots, tomatoes and herbs
boisson comprise	drink included
boisson gazeuse au gingembre	ginger ale/beer
boissons	drinks
boissons alcooliseés	alcoholic drinks
boissons sans alcool	non-alcoholic drinks
boitelle	poached in white wine with mushrooms

bolets	boletus mushrooms
bombe	small ice mould of eggs and whipped cream
bombe favorite	a lightly frozen meringue/cream and kirsch mould surrounded by melba sauce
bombe (glacée)	ice cream of two different flavours
bombe patricienne	a vanilla ice-cream filled with coffee mixture
bombe mascotte	mould lined with peach ice and centre filled with kirsch mixture
bombine	pork casseroled with layers of mushrooms or capers and potatoes - an ardèche speciality
bonbon fourré	soft centre
bonite (à dos rayé)	bonito (fish)
bordeaux	claret (wine)
bordelaise	red wine and shallot sauce. Poached bone marrow is often added
bordelaise (à la)	usually indicates the dish includes mushrooms
botargo	dish using tuna roe
bottereaux	liquer flavoured pastry fritters
bouchée	small rounds of puff pastry baked with centres removed ready for fillings (sweet or savoury)
bouchée à la reine	i) pastry shell traditionally filled with creamed sweetbreads and mushrooms
	ii) chicken vol-au-vent
bouchon	cork
boudin (blanc)	white pudding (white sausage USA)
boudin (noir)	black pudding (blood sausage USA)
boudoir	sponge finger/trifle sponge
bouffi	kippered herring
bouillabaise	marseilles speciality - fish and seafood stew/scorpion fish often used
bouillade	sauce of sweet pepper, garlic and wine
bouillinade des pêcheurs	fish soup
bouilli	boiled
bouillie	maize meal porridge, traditionally served with soup or stews
bouillon cube	stock cube
bouillon de poule	thin chicken soup
boule de neige	i) little round sponge cake/ice cream covered in whipped cream
	ii) wild mushroom
boules au choix (2)	scoops of your choice of ice cream (2)

boulette	meat ball
boumanio	purée of aubergine (egg plant USA) with cream
bouquet	prawns
bouquet garni	mixture of herbs and vegetables tied together and used in white stock
bourdaloue	hot poached fruit with vanilla custard, crushed macaroons, apricot and kirsch sauce
bourdelot de poires	baked pear dumpling
bourgeoisie (à la)	cooked with carrots, onions and bacon
bourgogne	burgundy (wine)
bourguiginonne	red wine and herb sauce
bourigoule	mushroom
bourrache	borage
bourride	a marseilles speciality - fish stew with garlic mayonnaise
bourriols	buckwheat yeast pancakes
boutargue	paste of dried salted mullet or tuna roe
boutefas	pork sausage
bouteilles (en)	bottled
boutifare	black pudding of bacon and herbs
braisé	braised
bramafan (salade)	artichoke stuffed with mushrooms, scampi and walnuts
brandade (de morue)	a creamy paste of salt cod with olive oil, milk and garlic
brayaude de mouton	boiled leg of mutton
bréjauda	bacon and cabbage soup
brème	bream (fresh water)
brème de mer	black sea bream
brési	smoked beef
bresolles/brézolles	slices of veal/beef/mutton baked with white wine and shallots (ham and mushrooms)
bretonne (à la)	dish usually with white haricot beans
brézolle	thick escalope of veal
brézolles/bresolles	moulded and sliced (usually veal) layered with onions, ham and mushrooms
brick	fritter (with a filling)
brigoule	mushroom
brioche	small fluted cottage loaves
brique-rose	tomato and meat sauce
broccana	veal/pork meat pasty

broche (à la)	food roasted on a spit
brochet de mer	barracuda (fish)
brochet	pike
brocheton	young pike
brochette (en)	kebab (served on a skewer)
brouffade	marinaded beef with anchovies, capers and gherkins
brouillés	scrambled (eggs)
broye	cornmeal porridge
brugnon	nectarine
brune	a rich brown sauce
brune/blonde	dark/light
brunoise	a garnish as in julienne, but the vegetables are cut into the smallest possible dice before being cooked
brut	very dry
bruxelloise (à la)	dish with brussel sprouts and chicory
buccin	whelk
bûche au chocolat	chocolate swiss roll
bûche de noël	yule log
buisson	food (fish/shellfish) piled up in a dish
bulot	whelk

C

cabillaud	cod
cabri	kid goat
cacahouètes/cacahuètes	peanuts
café	coffee
café décaféiné	decaffinated coffee
café de paris	a cognac and herb flavoured butter sauce
café moulu	finely ground coffee
café nature	black coffee
café noir/au lait/crème	black coffee/with milk/with cream
caille	quail
caillebotte	curds, eaten fresh
caillette	rennet, stomach
caillettes	chopped pork mixed with spinach, herbs and puréed potatoes and fashioned into faggot-shapes

caillettes de cornouaille	faggot-shaped meatballs served with a spicy sauce
caladons	crisp orange biscuits
calmar	squid
calvados	apple-distilled brandy (liquer)
camarguaise (à la)	a dish with all or some of the following:- tomato, herbs, garlic, black olives, orange peel, wine and brandy
canapés	small round fried bread, cheese or shortcrust pastry covered with a savoury mixture/served hot or cold
canard	duck
canard à la rouennaise	stuffed duck with liver
canard laqué	peking duck
canard sauvage	wild duck
canard siffleur	widgeon
canard/caneton á l'orange	most famous french duck dish - braised with oranges/orange liquer
canardeau	duckling
cancalaise (à la)	a sauce of oysters/shrimps with cream and whitewine
cancale	oyster
caneton	i) duckling ii) served in a "napkin" eg rice, jacket potato
canette	duckling (female)
canneberges	cranberries
cannelle	cinnamon (stick)
cannelon	savoury puff pastry cone
cantarèu(x)	grey snails
canteloup	large melon with soft orange sweet flavoured flesh
capoum	provençal name for hogfish or rascasse
câpres	capers
capucine	nasturtium
caquelon	small earthenware dish
carafe	carafe
caraïbe	caribbean cabbage
caramel au beurre	butterscotch/toffee
carapace	shell
caraque	chocolate sponge cake

carbonnade flamande	belgian originality - slices of braised beef and onions in beer
carbonnades	thin slices of pork (usually braised)
cardamome	cardamom
cardinal	a fish-stock based sauce made with lobster, butter, milk (and possibly chopped truffles)
cardon	cardon, a little known vegetable in england very similar to artichoke family - sliced and boiled (often served with other vegetables)
cardons à la moelle	cardoons in white sauce
cari	curry or curry sauce
caroline	small savoury pastry
carottes	carrots
carottes à la vichy	glazed carrots
carpaccio	marinated raw beef or fish
carpe	carp (fish)
carré d'agneau	rack of lamb
carré de porc	loin of pork
carrelet	i) plaice ii) flounder
carte (à la)	a list of dishes with prices shown
carvi	caraway
cassata	various shaped ice moulds (several ice flavours used) nuts/candied fruits added
casse-croûte	snacks
cassis	I) blackcurrant liqueur (often mixed with white wine) ii) blackcurrants
cassonade	soft, light brown sugar
cassoulet (toulousain)	casserole consisting of haricot beans, mutton or salt pork/sausages and preserved goose
catalan(e) (à la)	dish with tomatoes, garlic, onions and perhaps peppers, aubergines, rice or chick peas
caviar	the salted roe of the sturgeon or sterlet fish
cebiche	marinaded fish (usually red snapper, cod or haddock)
céleri	celery
célerirave	celeriac
cèpage	vine (plant)
cèpe	flap mushrooms
céréale	cereal

cerf	venison (red deer)
cerfeuil	chervil
cerises (noires)	cherries (black)
cervelas	large, short pork sausage, similar to saveloy
cervelas de brochet	a pike and potato sausage
cervelle	brains
cervelle de veau	calves brains
cervoise	barley beer
ceviche	dish with raw hake
chair	flesh/pulp of fruit
chair à saucisse	sausagemeat
champagne	champagne
champignons (de paris)	button mushrooms
champignons bordelaises	mushrooms cooked in grape juice
champignons de couche	cultivated mushrooms
champignons roses de champs	wild mushrooms
champignons sauvages	wild mushrooms
champigny	small puff pastry filled with apricot jam
chanoinesses	honey cake
chapeau	pie crust
chapelet	string (of sausages)
chapelure	breadcrumbs
chapon	capon
charbonnée de touraine	liver and lungs in red wine and blood sauce
charcuterie	assorted pork meats
charcutière	a vinegar, white wine and pickles/gherkins sauce
chardon	thistle (wild)
charentais	a small sweet scented melon
chariot	trolley of hors d'oeuvres/desserts or cheeses
charlotte	a buttered bread mould, filled with fruit, usually served hot
charlotte brillat-savarin	charlotte filled with pears, flavoured with Kirsch and covered in apricot sauce
charlotte de pommes	a dish of cooked apple covered with crumbs of toast
charlotte russe	a custard or cream enclosed in a sponge cake
charolais	i) breed of cattle ii) dry goat's milk cheese
charteuse au citron	lemon jelly with grapes and cream

chartreuse	i) a mixture of fruit, meat or vegetables served as an entrée
	ii) a brandy based liqueur (yellow or green)
chasseur	cooked in white wine, mushrooms, tomato and herb sauce
châtaigne	sweet chestnut
châtaigne d'eau	water chestnuts
châteaubriand(t)	a thick piece of fillet (porterhouse steak), sufficient for 2 people, carved at time of serving
châtelaine (â la)	artichoke hearts filled with chestnut purée with braised lettuce and potato balls
chaudèus	orange-flavoured biscuits
chaud-froid	a dressing containing gelatine
chaudrée	fish chowder of conger eel, plaice, whiting and wine - a poitou-charente speciality
chausson	flaky/puff pastry turnover with sweet or savoury filling
chausson aux pommes	apple turnover
chemise	a wrapping - pastry, leaf etc.
chemise (en)	baked in grease proof paper
chevaine	chub (fish)
chevalier	char (fish)
cheveux d'ange	vermicelli
chevreau	young kid goat
chevreuil	i) venison (roe deer)
	ii) poivrade sauce with red wine added
chevreuil (en)	cooked like venison
chiche	chick pea
chicolle	peaches in red wine
chicon	chicory or cos lettuce
chicorée	endive/chicory
chien de mer	shark (small)
chiffonnade	shredded
chips	crisps (potato chips)
chocolat à cuire	cooking chocolate
chocolat (chaud) (froid)	chocolate drink (hot) (cold)
chocolats fourres à la crème	chocolate creams
choquart	cinnamon and apple pastry
choron	a tomato béarnaise sauce
chou (rouge)	(red) cabbage

chou à la crème	cream puff
chou brocolis	broccoli
chou cabus	white cabbage
chou de chine	chinese leaves
chou de mai	spring cabbage
chouée	cabbage and butter dish
chou frisé	kale
chou navet	swede
chou rave	kohlrabi
choucroute	german dish of pickled cabbage and smoked sausages
choucroute garnie	sauerkraut served with sausages/cured pork, fresh or smoked goose
chouée	green cabbage with butter and vinegar
chou-fleur	cauliflower
chou-fleur au gratin	cauliflower cheese
choux de bruxelles	brussel sprouts
choux de mer	sea kale
ciboule(tte)	spring onion (chives)
citron (pressé)	lemon (juice)
citron vert	lime
citronelle	lemon grass/balm
citronné	a taste or flavour of lemon
civelles	baby eels
civet	jugged/stewed
civet de lapin/lièvre	jugged rabbit/hare
clafouti(s)	a light fruit batter pudding invariably made with unstoned cherries
clarence	a curried cream sauce
clermont (à la)	a dish with chestnuts and onions, or with salt pork and cabbage rolls
clin d'oeil (d'épices)	a "twinkling" of spices
clous de girofle	cloves
clouté (e)	studded
clovisse	smooth shelled clam (golden carpetshell)
cochon de lait	suckling pig
cochons de mer	("sea-pigs") grey mullet, feeding in estuaries and tidal harbours
cocon	mushroom
cocotte (minute)	casserole dish (pressure cooker)
coeur	heart

coffre	body of lobster
coffret	pastry "caskets"
cognac	brandy
coing	quince
colin	hake
colinot	codling (fish)
collioure	an anchovy flavoured mayonnaise (garnished with shrimps)
colonel	(lemon) water ice doused with vodka
coloquinte	colocynth (type of gourd)
colvert	(wild) mallard duck
compote	stewed fruit
compote de pommes	stewed apples/apple sauce
concassé	ground/pounded/roughly chopped (usually refers to tomatoes)
concombre	cucumber
condé	i) name of old french family - several dishes in which rice forms an important ingredient ii) red beans (mashed)
condiment	seasoning
confit	i) crystalised fruit ii) conserve of goose/duck
confit au vinaigre	pickled
confit de canard	pieces of duck preserved in fat
confiture	jam
confiture d'oranges	marmalade
congre	conger eel
consommé	clear (meat) soup
consommé à l'oeuf	clear meat soup with a raw egg
consommé au porto	clear meat soup with port wine
contre filet	loin strip steak, thicker slices are grilled as t-bone or rump steaks
convercle en pâte	pastry lid
coq au chambertin	chicken in red wine (burgundy)
coq au vin	chicken casseroled in red wine and garlic
coq de bruyère	woodgrouse (large)
coque	i) shell/cockle ii) type of clam
coque (à la)	soft-boiled (eggs)
coques de meringues	meringue shells
coquillages	shellfish

coquilles en pâte	pastry scallop shells
coquilles st. jacques	scallops in a creamy mayonnaise sauce served on the half shell
corail	i) coral, (red part)
	ii) red sauce
corbeille	basket
coriandre	coriander
cornet de glace	ice cream cornet
cornets de murat	rolled wafer biscuits
cornets feuilletés	cream horns
cornichons	gherkins (pickles)
corniottes	triangles of puff pastry, shaped into cones and stuffed with savoury or sweet fillings
corniottes bourguignonnes	cheese feuilletés
cornouaillaise (à la)	cooked in cornish style
corquignoise	shellfish and spicy fish stew
corrolle	inner petals of a flower
corsé	full-bodied
côte	rib/chop
côte de boeuf	rib of beef/t-bone steak
côte de veau	veal cutlet
côtelette	chop
côtes de céleri	celery stalks
côtes de regord	lamb cutlets
cotriade bretonne	fish stew with sorrel and leek
cou	neck
cou d'oie farci	goose neck stuffed with pork and foie gras
couennes (de porc)	pork rinds (often used in stews)
coulemelle	mushrooms
coulibiac	fish/chicken mixture wrapped in brioche pastry and baked (hot)
coulis	a thick liquid purée of fruit or vegetables, (usually tomatoes), made without flour
coulis d'écrivisses	crayfish bisque (soup)
coulis de tomate	ripe tomatoes with onions/garlic puréed to create a rich red sauce
coup de jarnac	meringue, sponge with jam and cognac
coupe (glacée)	sundae
coupe jacques	lemon and strawberry ice cream with fruit steeped in kirsch
courge	marrow

courgette	courgette (zucchini)
couronne	crown
courquignoise	spicy fish and shellfish stew
courraye	cabbage stuffed with game (usually rabbit)
court bouillon	stock used for poaching fish
couscous	north african dish of steamed couscous with meat, vegetables etc.
cousinat	vegetable stew
cousinat à la bayonnaise	vegetable stew with ham
cousinette	veal/spinach/sorrel/lettuce soup
coustelou au feu de bois	barbecued spare-ribs
couteau	razor shell
crabe	crab
crapaudine (à la)	spatchcocked (fowl)
craquelin	i) cracker biscuit
	ii) apple-stuffed pastry
craquelot	grilled smoked herring
craterelle	horn of plenty mushroom
crécy	dishes generally connected with carrots (often in purée form)
crème	whipped cream/butter/custard creams to garnish pastries and cakes, custard cream sauces and soups
crème (à la)	a dish accompanied by cream or cream sauce
crème à la vanille	light custard
crème anglaise	custard
crème anglaise au câfé	coffee-flavoured custard
crème argenteuil	cream of asparagus soup
crème bachique	a wine and egg custard
crème bourdaloue	a cream consisting of milk, eggs, sugar and ground almonds
crème brûlée	rich cream or custard base topped with caramelized sugar
crème caramel	vanilla-flavoured custard surrounded with soft caramel
crème chantilly	whipped cream
crème chantilly flan	whipped cream custard
crème/citron	served with milk/lemon
crème comtesse	cream of asparagus soup
crème d'asperges	cream of asparagus soup
crème d'orge	cream of barley soup

crème de bolets	cream of mushroom soup
crème de citron	lemon curd
crème de maís	cornflour
crème volaille	cream of chicken soup
crème épaisse	double cream
crème fleurette	lightly whipped single cream
crème fouetée	whipped cream
crème fraîche	a thick dairy or fresh cream with nutty, slightly cheesy flavour
crème frangipane	an almond, rum-flavoured thick cream
crème glacée	ice cream
crème gruyère	cheese spread
crème pithiviers	an almond, rum-flavoured thick cream
crème renversée	custard cream/mould
crème saint-honoré	filling for choux puffs and pancakes. A light, liquer-flavoured cream
crème st. germain	a soup consisting of cabbage, onions, peas
crémets d'angers	moulded fresh cheese
crémeux (euse)	creamy
créole (à la)	a dish with rice, sweet peppers and tomatoes
crépaze	pancake layered with ham and cream, sprinkled with cheese
crêpe	thin pancake with a variety of fillings
crêpe pralinées	warm thin pancake lined with almonds and rum mixture
crêpes dentelles	wafer thin crêpes, served rolled
crêpe suzette	thin, large pancakes, simmered in orange juice/flambéd with orange liqueur
crépinette	small highly seasoned flat sausage, usually grilled or fried
crespeou	small fish dipped in flour and shallow fried
cresson	watercress
crêtes de coq	cocks comb
crevette gris	small shrimp (brown)
crevette grosse	large prawn
crevette royal	large prawn
crevettes (roses)	shrimps (common prawn)
crique	grated potatoes mixed with garlic and parsley, shaped into flat cakes and shallow fried
crispés de montignac	small egg croquettes, with tomato sauce

croquant(e)	i) crisp/crunchy
	ii) almond petit four
	iii) honey biscuit
croquants orléanais	crisp nut cakes
croquembouches	pyramid of choux pastries
croque monsieur	toasted cheese and ham sandwich
croquette	rissole/croquette
crottin de chavignol	goats milk cheese
croustade	pastry/bread/potato shell usually with savoury filling
croustille	i) crispy
	ii) very thinly sliced fried potato
croûte	bread, pie crust or cheese rind
croûte au fromage	melted cheese served on a slice of toast or fried bread, open topped with ham and/or fried egg
croûtes dijonnaise	palmier cakes served with blackcurrant liquer and covered with chantilly-flavoured cream
croûtes à la moelle	beef marrow on toast
croûton	fried small cubes of bread, served with cream or puréed soups
cru	raw - uncooked
cruchades	fried cornmeal cakes
crudités	mixed raw vegetable salad
crudités niçoises	large platter of raw vegetables with dips served separately
crustacés	crustaceans (i.e. shrimps, lobsters, crabs i.e. shellfish)
cuiller/cuillère	spoon/spoonful
cuiller/cuillère à café	coffee/teaspoon
cuiller/cuillère à soupe	soup spoon
cuisse	thigh/drumstick
cuisse de poulet	chicken leg/drumstick
cuisseau	leg of veal
cuisses de grenouilles	frogs' legs
cuit	cooked
cuit à la vapeur	steamed
cuit à l'eau	boiled
cuit à petit feu	cooked slowly/simmered
cuit au four	baked
culotte (de boeuf)	rump (of beef)
cumin	caraway

curaçao	a bitter orange liqueur
curcuma	turmeric

D

daguet	young stag
dariole	a small narrow mould, used to set creams and jellies and to bake certain desserts (savoury or sweet)
darne	fish steak/thick slice cut across the body
dartois	a tart with layers of flaky pastry
dattes	dates
daube	traditionally a beef dish, either cut into square pieces or thick escalopes and cooked in red wine (chicken and game are sometimes used)
daurade	gilt head sea bream
décortiqué	shell/husk removed
déjeuner	lunch
délice	delight, delightful
délice aux amandes	chocolate ice cream with chocolate sauce and almonds
délices de crabe	creamy crab in crisp-breaded crust
demi-bouteille	half bottle
demi-poulet grillé	half a roasted chicken
demi-sel	lightly salted
dent-de-lion	dandelion
dernier service	last sitting
désossé	with bones removed (meat)
dessert	dessert
diable	piquant wine, vinegar, tomato and pepper sauce
diane	highly peppered cream sauce
dinde	turkey (hen)
dindon	turkey (cock)
dindonneau	young turkey (cock)
diots	small sausages
diplomate	trifle
dius	sliced potatoes cooked in the oven
dorade commune	red bream

dorade gris	black bream
doré	i) glazed (cake)
	ii) browned (meat)
dorée	john dory (fish)
dorer	to brown food lightly
double-crème	cream cheese
douceur	sweetness
douillon	i) wrapped in pastry
	ii) whole pear wrapped in pastry
douillon de pommes	baked apple dumpling
doux	sweet
dragée	sugared almond
drageés	sweet meats made of fruits/nuts covered with a coating of sugar icing
dubary	dish/soup with cauliflower (with mornay sauce as accompaniment)
duchesses de rouen	macaroons
duglére	fish sauce with cream, tomatoes, chives and parsley
dur	hard (boiled)
duxelles	i) chopped mushrooms and shallots with seasoning
	ii) sauce with mushrooms

E

eau (au siphon)	water (soda water siphon)
eau (chaude) (froide)	(hot) (cold) water
eau -de-vie	brandy (plum etc.)
eau douce	fresh water
eau gazeuse	fizzy (carbonated) water
eau minérale	mineral water
eau plate	still, plain water
écaille	scale/shell
écaillé	scaled (fish)
écale	shell (nut)
échalote	shallot
échine	chine or loin (usually pork)

écorce	bark (of cinnamon)
écorce d'orange	candied orange
écorce de citron	lemon peel
écrevisses	crayfish
écrin	pastry case
effiloché	"frayed" often describes preparation of vegetables
églefin	haddock
embeurré	buttered
embeurré de chou	cabbage boiled with butter
émiettée	crumble
émincé	strips/finely sliced/shredded (vegetables)
enchaud	a casseroled loin of pork with pigs' trotters, vegetables and spices. The pork is studded with garlic
enchaud périgourain	roast loin of pork with garlic
enchaud périgourdin	roast rolled fillet of pork
encornet	squid
encre de seiche (l')	cuttlefish ink
endives belges	chicory
enrobé de légumes	in vegetable coats
entrecôte	rib or rib-eye steak (beef) sometimes a slice from the rump is served under this name
entrecôte bordelaise	steak covered in an onion and red wine sauce
entrecôte marchand de vin	steak in red wine sauce
entrées	main dish of meal
entremets	dainty dishes usually served as hot or cold sweets
eouyat	apple dumpling
épaule	shoulder
éperlans	smelt (fish)
épi	bread, shaped like ear of wheat
épicé	spicy (dish)
epigramme	cutlets/slices of breast dipped in eggs and breadcrumbs and fried or grilled
épinards	spinach
épinards en branche	whole spinach
épine	vinette-barberry
équille	sand eel
escabeche	chilled fish dish, pilchard or herring fillets, in a piquant tomato sauce
escalope	i) cutlet/scallop ii) thin slice of fresh meat or fish

escargots	snails
escargots à la caudéran	snails in garlic-shallot sauce, scented with pernod and garnished with ham and herbs
escauton de voilaille	chicken breasts
espadon	swordfish
espagnole	a rich brown sauce consisting of meat stock and vegetables, white wine and tomato purée
esquinado toulonais	gratin of crabmeat and mussels
estofinado	salt cod and potatoes shredded/mashed and mixed together
estouffade	a meat (usually pork and turkey) casserole, stewed in a sealed pot with wine, herbs and vegetables
estouffade de boeuf	braised beef
estragon	tarragon
estuire	estuary
étouffée (à l')	stewed
étrangère	foreign
etrille	velvet swimming crab
étuvée	i) steamed (vegetables) ii) braised (meat)
éventail (en)	fan-shaped
express	espresso coffee

F

faisan	pheasant
faisan à l'alsacienne	pheasant cooked with sauerkraut
faisan à l'américaine	pheasant grilled with tomatoes, mushrooms and bacon
faisan à l'angoumoise	pheasant roasted and stuffed with truffles
faisan à la bohémienne	pheasant casseroled with foie gras, truffles and paprika
faisan à la languedocienne	pheasant casseroled with ham, mushrooms, truffles and alcohol
faisan à la normande	pheasant casseroled with apples, cream and calvados
faiselle	basket/pot for cheese

faïnes normandes	flat cinnamon cakes
falue	sweet pancake
fanfre	pilot fish/similar to mackerel
faon	fawn/young deer
far breton	prune flan
farce(ie)e(s)	stuffing
farcement	potatoes baked with milk, eggs and sometimes raisins, bacon and prunes
farcidure	i) wholewheat pancakes with bacon
	ii) buckwheat dumpling
farçon	i) large fried sausage and vegetable cake
	ii) potatoes baked with eggs and milk
	iii) large saveloy sausage
farée	stuffed cabbage
farigoule(tte)	wild thyme
farine	flour
farine d'avoine	oat meal
faubonne- (potage)	i) white haricot bean soup
	ii) split pea soup
fausse daurade	sea bream (red)
fausse limande	scald fish (flat sea fish)
fausse palourde/praire	small clam
faux mousseron	scotsman bonnet, an aromatic yellow, thin mushroom
faux-filet	sirloin of meat (usually beef or pork)
favouilles	small crabs
fenouil	fennel
fenouillet	pear (aniseed taste)
fenugrec	fenugreek
féra	fresh water (lake) salmon
fermentée	fermented
fermière (à la)	served with mixed vegetables
ferrecapienne	fish soup
ferval	garnish of artichokes and croquette potatoes
feuille de chêne	red oak-leaf lettuce
feuille de laurier	bay leaf
feuille de vigne	vine leaf
feuilles vertes	green leaves (often refers to lettuce etc.)
feuilleté ésolognote	feuilleté of game
feuilletons	small crescent-shaped pieces of puff pastry
féverole	field bean

féves	broad beans
féves à la tourangelle	beans with ham
fiatole	delicate mediterranean fish
ficelle	thinner loaf than baguette
ficelle normande/picarde	pancake stuffed with cream/cheese/ham or mushrooms
fichu	"coated"/wrapped
figue de barbarie	prickly pear
figues	figs
filet	i) a prime cut of meat/fish, all bones removed
	ii) fillet steak (tenderloin USA)
	iii) loin of lamb
filet mignon	centre filet of meat trimmed into a triangular shape
filtrer	to filter/percolate
financière	a sauce comprising of truffles, olives, mushrooms and madeira wine
fine de claire	oyster raised in a special basin
fines herbes	mixture of mixed herbs
fiouse lorraine	fresh cheese tart
fistulane	small shellfish
fistuline	large/red sourish mushroom
flageolets	small kidney beans
flagnarde	i) sweet flan
	ii) thick jam pancake
flamande (à la)	stewed with vinegar, apples and sugar
flambé (e)	i) singed poultry or game (usually set alight at table)
	ii) a pudding pancake or omelette served covered with spirit and set alight
flamiche au maroillès	cheese tart (similar to gouda)
flamiche picarde	leek pie - a picardy speciality
flamri	usually cold semolina pudding served with puréed raw red fruits
flanchet	flank of beef, used in stews
flaugnarde	i) sweet flan
	ii) thick jam pancake
flaugnard limousine	baked custard flan/tart
flavou (ille)	type of crab
flétan	halibut/flounder
fleuriste - (à la)	garnish of stuffed tomatoes and potatoes

fleurons	small crescent-shaped pieces of puff pastry used for garnish/or coated with sauce
fleurs	flower (shapes)
flie	small clam
floc de gascogne	aperitif of grape juice and armagnac
flocons de maïs	corn flakes
flognarde	i) sweet flan
	ii) thick jam pancake
flon	golden custart tart
florentine	i) a sauce with spinach
	ii) chocolate coated biscuit of nuts, candied fruit and toffee
florentine (à la)	dish served on a bed of spinach and usually covered with cheese sauce
florian	garnish of braised lettuce/carrots, onions and potatoes
flute	long thin loaf of french bread
foie	liver
foie de boeuf	mushroom
foie de veau à l'anglaise	bacon and grilled calf's liver
foie de veau moissonnière	calf's liver in tomato and wine sauce
foie gras	only fattened goose or duck liver is used for this fine paté
foin d'artichaut	choke (of artichoke)
fond blanc de veau	white veal stock
fond brun de veau	brown veal stock
fond de moules	mussel stock
fond de poisson	fish stock
fond de volaille	chicken stock
fondue	hot bubbly mixture of melted cheese or savoury sauce, white wine, a drop of kirsch and garlic. A bite-size piece of bread is dipped into the pot (a swiss speciality)
fondue bourguignonne	meat fondue
forestière	a sauce with mushrooms
forestière (à la)	dish with mushrooms, bacon and potatoes
formenteau	table grape
fort	strong
fouetée	whipped e.g. cream etc.
fougasse	crisp flat loaves from the south of france
foulque	coot (water bird)
fourée	stuffed/lined
fournitures	salad greens and herbs

fourré(e)	stuffed
fourrés	fritters
frais	fresh
fraise marquise	strawberries soaked in kirsch with whipped cream and strawberry purée
fraises	strawberries
fraises de bois	wild strawberries
fraisier	strawberry cake
framboises	raspberries
française (à la)	i) garnish of potato nests filled with vegetables ii) dish cooked in butter
françoise	a piquant mayonnaise
francolin	type of partridge
frangipane	a pastry filled with cream and flavoured with almonds
frappé	i) chilled (wine) ii) milkshake
fréneuse	a purée of creamed turnips and potatoes
fretin	young fish
freux	rook
friand salé	savoury meat pie in puff pastry
friand sucré	almond biscuit/cookie
friandise	sweetmeat, titbit
friands	savoury meal rolls
fricadelle	meatball
fricandeau	i) gently cooked/braised joint of meat ii) topside of meat, usually veal iii) slice of large fish
fricandelle	fried minced meatball (usually beef)
fricassé	a dish of fowl, rabbit etc. cut into pieces and served in white sauce
fricassée	meat (most often chicken or veal) sautéed and lightly stewed. Served in cream sauce
fricoté	stewed
frigolet	wild thyme
frisée	i) curly (e.g. lettuce) ii) endive
frit	fried
fritot	savoury fritters made with small pieces of marinated meat and poultry, served with tomato sauce as hors d'oeuvres

fromage	cheese (see separate section on cheeses)
fromage à la crème	cream cheese
fromage à pâte molle	soft cheese
fromage à tartiner	cheese spread
fromage battue	mild cream cheese
fromage blanc	slightly salted fresh soft cream cheese
fromage chèvre	goat's milk cheese
fromage cuit	cooked fresh cream cheese
fromage de brebis	sheep's milk cheese
fromage de tête	brawn/boiled, chopped and moulded
fromage de vache	cow's milk cheese
fromage fondu	processed cheese
fromage frais	medium fat, smooth cheese (cows milk) - yoghurt consistency
froment	wheat
fruit à pain	bread fruit
fruit secs	dried fruit
fruitée	cold fruit sauce (if simmered, resembles british cumberland sauce)
fruits	fruit
fruits de mer	seafood
fruits des bois	wild mushrooms
fruits rafraîchis	fruit salad
fumé	smoked
fumet	aroma/bouquet/flavour/essence of game/fish
fumet de poisson	fish stock
fumoir	smoking room

G

gâche	flat yeast bread
gaillarde/gribiche	cold vinaigrette with hard boiled egg yolks, capers and gherkins
galantines	cold jellied mould of boned poultry or fish
galathée	prawn
galetou	thick pancake made with buckwheat flour
galette	buckwheat pancake/girdle cake/open tart
galette d'avoine	oat-cake

galicien	rich pistachio-flavoured cake
galimafrée à la vauban	shoulder of lamb stuffed with chopped lamb, mushrooms, garlic and herbs
galopins	bread pancakes
gamba	large prawn
garbure	cabbage and vegetable soup - with salt pork/preserved goose, beans and garlic
garbure béarnaise	pork stew with vegetables and confit
gardon	roach
gargouillau	i) pear cake
	ii) pears baked in batter
garniture	i) garnish/topping
	ii) served with vegetables
garniture au choix	choice of vegetable accompaniment
gasconnade	roast leg of lamb with garlic and anchovies
gâteau(x)	cake(s)
gâteau au chocolat	chocolate cake
gâteau bretonne	a flattish fruit cake
gâteau de châtaigne	chestnut gâteau
gâteau de pithviers	feuilleté with almond filling
gâteau fourré	cream filled cake
gâteau glacé périgourdine	ice cream gateau with walnut and chocolate truffles
gâteau marjolaine	layers of nut flavoured meringue and chocolate cream
gâteau sévillan	orange cake
gâteau st. honoré	choux cream puff-balls
gatis	cheese served hot in a brioche crust
gauffre	waffle
gaufre	thin biscuit wafer, baked or fried
gazeux	fizzy (drink)
gelée (en)	jelly (jellied)
gendarme	i) salted smoked herring
	ii) dry sausage
genevoise	a fish stock and red wine sauce served chiefly with trout and salmon
genièvre	juniper berries
gentiane	mountain flower (used for flavouring of liquers)
gentilhomme (potage)	game and lentil soup
georgette(pommes de terre)	potatoes stuffed with crayfish tails
georgette (potage)	globe artichoke soup

germes de luzerne	alfafa sprouts
germes de soja	beansprouts/bean shoots
germon	tuna (white tunny fish)
gibier	game
gibier à plumes	game birds
gibier à poil	game animals
gibier d'eau	wildfowl
gibolette	stew, usually rabbit
gigot	leg (lamb)
gigot d'agneau à la bretonne	leg of lamb with white beans and tomatoes
gigot de mer	monkfish/angler fish
gigot de sept heures	braised leg of lamb (cooked for six or seven hours) with garlic
gigu (e)	i) haunch of venison
	ii) haunch of wild boar
gimblette	ring biscuit
gingembre	ginger
gin-tonic	gin and tonic
girelle	rainbow wrasse (mediterranean fish)
girofle	clove
girolle	chanterelle mushroom
gironnaise (à la)	dish served with a cream, mustard and gherkin sauce
gîte à la noix	silverside/topside of beef
givré	frosty (of cake)
glaçage	icing
glacé(e)	glazed/iced (of cake)/frozen; ice cold
glace	ice cream
glace armenonville	a hot chocolate sauce with coffee and vanilla ice cream
glace aux fraises/ à la vanille	strawberry/vanilla ice-cream
glace madeleine	a kirsch soaked crystallised pineapple mixed with vanilla ice cream and cream
glace panachée	a mixture of different flavoured ice cream
glacé royale	royal icing
glaçon	ice cube
glaire	white of an egg
glandoulat	casseroled garlic pork with carrots and red beans
gnocchi	dumplings of choux paste/semolina/potatoes

gogues	sausages
goguette	flat, highly spiced pork sausage
gombos/gombaut	okra/ladies fingers
goret	young pig
gougeas de quercy	small baked pumpkin puddings
gougère	choux pastry filled with gruyère cheese
goujon	gudgeon (small fresh water fish)
goujons	small strips of fish coated in flour and deep fried
gounerre	a type of potato pâté
gousse	shell/pod/husk
gousse d'ail	clove of garlic
goût	taste
goyave	guava
grain	berry
grain de cassis	blackcurrant
grain de raisin	grape
grain d'orge	barley corn
graine d'anis	aniseed
graines de carvi	caraway seeds
graines de pavot	poppy seeds
graines de sésame	sesame seeds
graisse de rognon	suet
grand-duc	asparagus/crayfish tails/truffles garnish with cheese sauce
grandmère	dish cooked with onions, mushrooms, bacon and potatoes
grand veneur	red wine/redcurrant, cream and pepper sauce
gras	fat
gras double	tripe and onions
gratin (au)	i) cooked with grated cheese ii) a dish grilled/baked with crisp brown crust (usually breadcrumbs or grated cheese)
gratin dauphinois	sliced potatoes baked with cream and browned on top - cheese and eggs may also be added
gratinée au porto	onion soup with port wine
gratinée aux oignons	french onion soup with toasted bread and cheese
gratin languedocien	baked aubergines, tomatoes and herbs
gratin savoyard	sliced potatoes cooked/baked in milk and cheese
grattons/gratterons	french equivalent of scratchings, small pieces of pork - skin cooked until crisp and golden
gravette	flat oyster

grecque (à la)	vegetables stewed with oil and herbs
grelette	cold whipped cream sauce
gremille	pope/ruff (small freshwater fish)
grenache	type of red wine grape
grenade	pomegranate
grenadier	sea fish
grenadin	small, thick square or triangular slice of meat or poultry (usually veal)
grenadine	bright red syrup
grenadins au poivre vert	medallions of veal, marinaded in cognac and cooked in a white wine and green peppercorn sauce
grenobloise (à la)	dish fried in butter, with capers and lemon
grenouille	frog
gressin	bread stick
gribiche/gaillarde	cold vinaigrette with hard boiled egg yolks, capers and gherkins
grignan	liqueur similar to chartreuse
grillade à la champagneules	french version of welsh rarebit - fried ham on toast, covered with a cheese sauce
grillades	grilled meat
grillé	grilled
grillé au charbon de bois	barbecued
griotte	morello cherry
griset	black sea bream
grisotte	parasol mushroom
grive	thrush
grondin	gurnard/gurnet (fish)
groseilles (rouges)	redcurrants
groseilles à maquereaux	gooseberries
gros mollet	lumpfish
gros sel (à)	baked in salt
gryphée	portuguese oyster
guigne	variety of cherry
guignolet	cherry liquer
guimauve	i) marshmallow ii) wild marshmallow plant
guyot	variety of pear
gymnètre	long flat mediterranean fish

H

habit vert (en)	wrapped in green leaf (e.g. cabbage)
hachau de veau	veal stew with ham, garlic and peppers
haché	chopped/minced meat
hachée	a tomato sauce with vinegar, capers, ham and mushrooms
hacher menu	to chop up small/mince
hachis parmentier	shepherd's pie
haddock	smoked haddock
halbran	young wild duck
halicot de mouton	mutton stew with turnips and onions
hampe (cerf) (boeuf)	breast (deer) flank (beef)
hareng	herring
hareng roulé	roll-mop herring
hareng salé	salt herring
haricot d'espagne	runner bean
haricot de mer	wedge-shelled clam
haricots blancs	haricot beans (white kidney beans)
haricots verts	french (green) beans
helvelle	fungi of various shapes
hochepot	oxtail, meat and vegetable stew
hollandaise	a sauce consisting of egg yolks, butter, vinegar or lemon juice (a basis for many other sauces)
homard	lobster
homard à l'américaine	diced, sautéed lobster, flamed in cognac, wine, aromatic vegetables/herbs and tomatoes
homard à la parisienne	lobster served cold with mayonnaise
homard à la russe	lobster served cold with mayonnaise
homard thermidor	lobster meat with a wine/shallot sauce and grated cheese, grilled and served in shells
hongroise	sauce of shallots, paprika, tomatoes and cream
hors d'oeuvre	starter (appetizer)
hors d'oeuvres variés	assorted appetizers
huile	oil
huile d'arachides	groundnut oil
huile de colza	rape seed oil
huile d'oillette	poppy seed oil
huile d'olive (vierge)	olive oil (virgin-top quality)
huile de tournesol	sunflower seed oil

huîtres	oysters
hure	head (often boar)
hussarde	creamy white sauce
hussarde (à la)	served with stuffed potatoes, mushrooms with onion purée, aubergines and horseradish
hydne	different coloured mushrooms
hysope	hyssop

I

igname	yam
île flottante	sponge cake steeped in kirsch, jam layers, covered with whipped cream
impériale	variety of plum
indienne (à l')	curry sauce (often served with rice)
iode	iodine
isigny	egg and butter sauce
italienne	a brown sauce of onions, mushrooms and white wine with or without ham
italienne (à l')	tomato/paste main ingredient of dish

J

jacques	apple pancakes
jalousie	small flaky pastry cake with strips, revealing fruit or jam
jamble	limpet
jambon	ham
jambon blanc	boiled ham
jambon de bayonne	bayonne ham, mildly smoked and cured in wine mixture
jambon de campagne/ montagne/pays	locally salted or smoked ham
jambon de paris	raw, smoked, delicately flavoured ham

jambonneau	cured pig's knuckle
jambonneau de volaille	leg of chicken
jardinière (à la)	fresh garden vegetables
jarret	knuckle (of veal) shin (of beef)
jau au sang	chicken in blood-thickened sauce
jaunotte	mushroom
jean-doré	john dory (fish)
jesse	freshwater fish similar to carp
jésus	large smoked pork liver sausage (sometimes dried)
jets de houblon à la crème	hop shoots in cream
joinville	rich cream, shrimps, or crayfish sauce
joue de boeuf	ox cheek
joues (de lotte)	cheeks (fish)
julienne	i) ling (fish)
	ii) very thinly sliced vegetables (matchstick size)
jus	juice from meat or game after cooking
jus (au)	dish dressed with own juice or gravy
jus (d'orange etc.)	juice (orange etc.)
jus de fruits	fruit juice
jus de pamplemousse	grapefruit juice
jus de pomme	apple juice
jus de tomate	tomato juice
jus de viande	gravy (meat)

K

kir	dry chilled white wine mixed with a blackcurrant syrup
kirsch	black cherry distilled brandy
kiwi	kiwi
kumquat	kumquat

L

labre	wrasse (fish)
lactaire	mushroom
lagopède (d'écosse)	pyrenean grouse (red grouse)
lait	milk
lait (au)	cooked in milk
lait caille	junket
lait froid/chaud	milk cold/hot
laitance	soft herring roe
laite	soft herring
laitue	lettuce
laitue romaine	cos lettuce
lamproie	lamprey (river fish)
lamproie au sang	lamprey and leeks in red wine and blood sauce
langouste	spiny lobster
langoustines	dublin bay prawns /scampi often just grilled or poached in a court-bouillon/served with mayonnaise or aioli
langue	tongue
langue de boeuf	i) ox tongue ii) mushroom
langue de chat	thin long dry biscuit
languier	smoked pig's tongue
lantin	mushroom
lapereau	young rabbit
lapin	rabbit
lard	bacon/fat
lard maigre	streaky bacon
larme	tear-shaped
laurier	bay leaf
lavagnon	small clam
lavande	lavendar
laveret	pollan (a highly esteemed salmon-type fish)
léche	sliver, thin slice
le chef vous propose	the chef recommends ...
léger	light
légumes	vegetables
légumes du marché	mixed vegetables
lentilles	lentils

lentilles jaunes	yellow lentils
lépiote	mushroom
letchi	lichee
libre-service	self-service
lieu jaune	pollack (fish)
lieu noir	coley (fish)
lièvre	wild hare
limaçons à la suçarelle	snails in meat sauce
limande	dab (member of the plaice family)
limande sole	lemon sole
limon givrée	lemon filled with sorbet
limonade	lemonade
limousine (à la)	stuffed with cèpes and chicken livers
lingue	long thin fish similar to cod
liquer	liqueur
lit	bed
litchi	lichee
livèche	lovage
loche (de rivière)	loach (river fish)
loche de mer	rockling (sea fish)
lochoise	brandy, cream and onion sauce
lompe	lumpfish
longe	loin of veal/pork
lorgnette	rolled fillet of fish
lotte (de mer)	monkfish
lotte à la nage	monkfish in light wine sauce
lotte de rivière	freshwater burbot
loubine	grey mullet
loup de mer	sea bass
loup de mer au fenouil	sea bass on a bed of fennel (often set alight with alcohol)
loup marin	wolf fish
louquenkas	pork sausage with red pepper and garlic
louvine	sea bass
lyonnaise	sauce with onions
lyonnaise (à la)	lyonese style dish - often cooked with fried, shredded onions

M

macaron	macaroon
macédoine	mixture of vegetables or fruit salad served in syrup or set in jelly (large diced)
macédoine de fruits	fruit salad
macédoine de legumes	mixed vegetables
macédoine en boîte	fruit cocktail
macérer	to soak - a term generally applied only to fruit soaked in liqueur or syrup
mâche	corn salad/lamb's lettuce
macis	mace
macre	water chestnut
macreuse	i) wild duck ii) shoulder of beef
madeleine	i) small dariole-shaped cake coated with jam and covered in coconut ii) name of a pear
madère	i) madeira wine ii) sauce with madeira wine
madrilène	a strongly flavoured consommé with tomato and chicken stock
madrilène (à la)	tomato flavoured dish
maigre	thin/lean (meat)
maigre (au)	dishes prepared without meat
maigret/magret	fillet/breast of duck
maintenon	velouté sauce with tomatoes and mushrooms
maintenon (à la)	louis XIV's favourite - dishes usually consisting of something grilled in a paper case
maïs	sweet corn
maison (fait à la)	home-made
maître d'hôtel	a sauce of butter, parsley, and lemon juice
manchon	i) small almond ii) pasty iii) beef steak
mandarine	tangerine
mandarine givrée	tangerine ice, dressed inside the unbroken skin of a fresh tangerine
mange-tout	sugar pea

mangue	mango
manqué de pommes de terre	potato cake
maquereau	mackerel
maraichère	served with mixed vegetables
maraschino	delicate cherry flavoured liqueur
marasquin	maraschino cherry/liquer
marbré	striped sea bream
marbré (de filet)	marbled/mottled/veined
marc	husks, grounds, dregs
marc (eau-de-vie de)	spirit distilled from grape residue
marcassin	young wild boar
marcassin ardenaise	marinated wild boar with celeriac
marcellin	small almond pastry
marchand de vin	a red wine and shallot sauce
marée	seafood
marengo	chicken/veal dish with tomatoes, garlic and mushrooms
mariné	marinaded
marinière	a mussel broth thickened with egg yolks and white wine
marinière (à la)	cooked with shallots/white wine/herbs
marjolaine	marjoram
marmelade	marmalade
marmite	cooking pot
marmite bressan	poached chicken
marmite dieppoise	fish/shellfish stew, cooked with spices
maroilles	strong smelling/tasty cheese
marquise (à la)	i) garnish of foie gras, truffles and cream sauce
	ii) pineapple and strawberry water ice
marquisette	small chocolate log
marrons (glacé)	chestnuts (candied)
marseillaise (à la)	marseilles-style, cooked with tomatoes, garlic, onions, anchovies and olives
masillon	small almond tartlet
massepain	marzipan
matelote	i) a fish stew (often eel) cooked with white or red wine
	ii) a piquant wine sauce with mushrooms and baby onions
matelote d'anguilles	stewed eels in red wine sauce

matias	flat, savoury cake with onions, leeks and potatoes
matignon	mixed vegetable stuffing or garnish
matjes	slightly salted herring, fermented and eaten raw
mauve	mallow plant
mauvis	redwing
mazarines	dishes combining fillets of meat and forcemeat
médallions	i) small rounds of meat/fish fillet, (smaller than tournedos)
	ii) tenderloin steak (lamb/pork/veal)
melangé	tossed salad
mélasse	molasses, treacle
mélasse raffinée	golden syrup
mêlé cassis	brandy with blackcurrant liquer
méli-mélo	mixture/combination of ...
mélisse	lemon balm
melon	melon
melsat	large white sausage
menon	roast kid-goat
menouille	bacon stew with beans, onions and potatoes
menthe	mint
menthe anglaise, poivrée	peppermint
menthe verte	spearmint
menu à prix fixe	set menu
menu gibier	small game
merguez	spiced sausage
merise	wild cherry
merlan	whiting
merlu	hake
merluche	dried unsalted cod, stockfish
mérou	grouper (large sea-fish)
merveilles charentaises	cognac fritters
mesclun	young mixed green salad leaves e.g. cress, dandelion leaves, endive etc.
meunière	sauce of browned butter, parsley and lemon juice
meurette	(fresh water) fish stew made with red or white wine
mias bourbonnais	cherry and custard tart
mi-cuit	semi/halfcooked
miel	honey
miette	crumb
mignardise	dainty/petit four

mignons	i) small evenly cut rounds of meat/fish
	ii) very fine fillet steak
mignotte	i) small round fillet of lamb
	ii) coarsly ground white peppercorns
	iii) small poultry or game mousse
mijoté(e)	simmered/slowly cooked
mijoteuse	slow cooker
milanaise	macaroni
milanaise (à la)	i) food generally dipped in egg and breadcrumbs, mixed with parmesan cheese and fried in butter (often served with spaghetti)
	ii) vegetables browned with butter and grated cheese
millas	cornmeal porridge
millassou	cornmeal pudding with raisins
mille feuilles	fine layers of puff pastry
milliard de cérises	cherries fried in batter
minute	grilled/fried with butter, lemon juice and parsley
minute (à la)	dishes which are cooked in the quickest possible way
miques	giant dumplings often served with salt pork and vegetables
mirabeau (à la)	a garnish of anchovy butter/tarragon, olives and anchovy fillets
mirabelle	i) small yellow plum
	ii) clear plum spirit
mireille	a hollandaise sauce with basil and tomato purée
miriton	stew
miriton (de boeuf)	thinly sliced beef and onions stewed in white wine
mirlitons	almond and cream tartlets
mitonné	simmered/slow cooked
mitonné (boeuf)	stewed beef
mocha	cake (coffee/chocolate flavouring)
mode (à la)	dish cooked in the style of.......e.g. à la reine - in the queen's style
moelle	i) bone marrow (usually beef)
	ii) stalks of vegetables
moelleux	i) creamy, smooth
	ii) mellow (wine)
mojettes à la crème	fresh white beans with garlic and cream
moka	coffee sponge cake

mollet	soft (boiled)
monbazillac	sweet white wine
mondée	blanched
mont-blanc	puréed chestnut dessert, topped with whipped cream
mont-bry	small spinach and cheese cakes with cèpes in cream
montgolfier	fish stuffed and poached with a white mushroom and lobster sauce
montrouge	served with mushrooms in cream
morilles	morels (mushrooms)
morme	striped sea bream
mornay	a cheese sauce
mortadelle	thinly sliced large pork sausage - a bologna speciality
morue	salt cod
morue à la malouinaise	salt cod with potatoes and cream
morue pil-pil	salt cod with chillies and garlic
moscovite	white wine sauce with caviar
mou	soft
mouclade	mussels in cream sauce - a poitou-charante speciality
moule à manquer	shallow cake tin
moules	mussels
moules en écrin	deep fried pastry cases of mussels, shrimps and mushrooms - served with a wine and fish sauce
moules marinière	mussels cooked in their own juice with onions
mourtairol	chicken boiled with saffron
mousse au chocolat	chocolate pudding
mousseline	a mayonnaise with cream
mousseron faux	fairy ring mushroom
mousserons	wild mushrooms
mousseux	sparkling
moutarde	i) a mustard sauce
	ii) mustard
muge	grey mullet
mulet (gris)	grey mullet
murène	moray eel
mûre/baie de rouce	blackberry
mûres	mulberries/blackberries
muscade	nutmeg

muscadet	light dry white wine
muscat	a sweet white wine (also the grape producing it)
musette (en)	boned, rolled and braised
musseau	muzzle
mye	soft-shelled clam
myrtilles	bilberries/blueberries
mystère	ice cream in meringue, coated with nuts

N

nage (en)	cooked in court-bouillon (fish)
nantaise	vinegar sauce with shallots and gherkins
nantua	béchamel sauce with cream and crayfish
nappé de	topped with/coated with
natte	plaited loaf
naturelle	plain
navarin	lamb stew/casserole
navarin printanier	spring lamb
navets	turnips
navettes aux oeufs	lemon-flavoured oval cakes
navettes d'albi	pastry boats with raisins and whole almonds
nectar d'abricot	apricot juice
nectarine	nectarine
niçoise	served with tomatoes, garlic, anchovies, olives and capers
nid	nest/bed (usually of vegetables/dessert)
nids de pommes de terre	potato nests (similar to straw potatoes)
nigelle	black cumin
nivernaise	a white wine, garlic and butter sauce
noisette	i) hazelnut ii) a nut of butter - often cooked to a dark brown and sharpened by vinegar. Used principally for fish and brains
noisette de beurre	knob of butter
noisettes	boned cutlets/neatly trimmed round or oval shapes of fillet steak (½ inch /2 cm thick approx.)
noix	walnuts
noix de beurre	knob of butter

noix de brésil	brazil nut
noix de cajou	cashew
noix de coco	coconut
noix de grenoble	walnuts
noix (de) muscade	nutmeg
nominoë	soup with chestnuts, egg yolks and cream
nonette	spiced bun
nonnettes	little honey cakes with royal icing
normande	a fish stock based sauce with cooked mussels, prawns and langoustines
normande (à la)	dish with cream and with one or all of the following:- calvados, cider, apples - a normandy speciality
nôtre manière (à)	cooked in "house-style"
nouilles	noodles
nouilles à l'éncre	home made egg noodles with ink (black)
nouilles au safran	home made saffron noodles
nouilles aux oeufs frais	home made egg noodles
nouilles vertes	home made green noodles
nouzillards au lait	cream of chestnut soup
noyau	i) stone of a fruit
	ii) a peach or nectarine flavoured liqueur
nulle	light egg custard
nymphes	frogs' legs

O

oblade	type of sea bream
oeufs à la cantalienne	fluffy baked eggs with cheese
oeufs à la coque	soft-boiled eggs in the shell
oeufs à la diable	devilled eggs
oeufs à la neige	"snow eggs" with caramel sauce
oeufs à la tripe	hard boiled eggs with onions
oeufs au bacon	bacon and eggs
oeufs au jambon	ham and eggs
oeufs au plat	eggs baked/grilled in butter in a shallow dish
oeufs bénedictine	brandade de morue with poached eggs and hollandaise sauce

oeufs brouillés	scrambled eggs
oeufs du florentine	eggs with spinach and mornay sauce
oeufs durs	hard boiled eggs
oeufs en cocotte	baked eggs in ovenware pots
oeufs en gelée	soft boiled eggs, covered in aspic and decorated with mayonnaise
oeufs lorraine	baked eggs with cheese and bacon
oeufs mimosa	hard boiled eggs in a thick mayonnaise
oeufs mollets	soft-boiled eggs (shelled)
oeufs pochés	poached eggs
oeufs sur le plat mirabeau	individually baked eggs cooked with olives and anchovies
oie	goose
oignon	onion
oignonade	onion stew
oiseau (d'eau)	bird (waterfowl)
oison	young goose
olives	olives
olives farcies	stuffed olives
olives noires	black olives
olives vertes	green olives
olivette	queen scallop
omble (ombre) (chevalier)	char (type of salmon)
ombre écailles	grayling (fish)
omelette au fromage	cheese omelette
omelette au jambon	ham omelette
omelette aux champignons	mushroom omelette
omelette aux fines herbs	herb omelette
omelette nature	plain omelette
omelette norvégienne	baked alaska (dessert)
onglet	top of skirt (beef), often grilled with shallots
opéra	garnish or salad of chicken liver/asparagus tips, celery, gherkins and occasionally truffles
operne	small shellfish
orange	orange
orangeade	orangeade
orange givrée	orange skin filled with orange sorbet
ordinaire	ordinary/common
oreille	ear of pig/calf
oreille de chat/de judas	fungi of various shapes
oreille de mer	shellfish (ear-shaped)

oreillette	i) small pig's ear
	ii) sweet fritter with orange blossom
oreillettes	fried mushrooms
oreillon	small ear/ear-shaped
oreillons (d'abricots)	halved (apricots)
orge	barley
orge perlé	pearl barley
origan	oregano
orly	usually dishes with slices of meat or fish, dipped in rich batter and fried in fat
ormeau (x)	shellfish (ear-shaped)
oronge	caesar's mushroom
ortie	nettle
ortolan	ortolan bunting
os à moelle	marrowbone
oseille	sorrel
oublie	wafer
ouillade	a soup of beans, cabbage, potatoes, ham and pork (vegetables removed and served separately)
oulade	bacon, vegetables and dried bean soup
oursin	sea urchin
outarde	bustard (bird)
oyonnade	goose stew
oyonnade du bourbonnais	goose in red wine and blood sauce with bacon and baby onions

P

pacquage	barrelling (of salt-fish)
pageau	sea bream
pageot	type of sea bream
pagre commun	sea bream
pagure	hermit crab
paillarde	grilled veal escalope
paillardine	grilled veal escalope
paillettes d'oignons frits	crisp fried onion rings
pain	bread
pain à la reine	fish mousse (often pike)

pain bis	brown bread
pain blanc	white bread
pain complet	wholemeal bread
pain d'épice	gingerbread
pain de gènes	almond cake
pain de siegle	large flat country bread (rye flour)
pain grillé	toast
paleron	part of the shoulder (beef) (chuck steak USA)
paloise	a béarnaise sauce with chopped mint stems and leaves
palombe	wood pigeon
palourde	large clam (carpetshell) eaten raw
pamplemousse	grapefruit
panaché(e)	i) mixed (flavour) ii) shandy
panache de poisson	grilled mixed fish
panais	parsnip
pan bagna	french sandwich
panisse	fried chick pea or maize cake, eaten with sugar
pannequet	pancake/crêpe, often stuffed and covered in cheese sauce
panoufle	cut from sirloin (beef)
panure	breadcrumbs
papaye	paw-paw/papaya
papeton	corn on the cob
papeton d'aubergines	aubergine/egg plant baked with eggs and cheese
papillote (en)	literally an envelope - a wrapping of paper or foil
paquette	female lobster
parfait	frozen mixture of egg and sugar with whipped cream
parisienne	a velouté sauce with mushrooms, also known as sauce allemande
par les soins de	by courtesy of ...
parmentier	dish cooked with potato
parmentier (potage)	potato and leek soup
par nos soins	with our compliments
pastèque	watermelon
pastilla	lozenge/pastille shape
pastille au miel	honey drop
pastis	aniseed based drink
patate	sweet potato/yam

pâte à chou	choux pastry
pâte à frire	batter
pâte à pâté	french pie pastry
pâte (à tarte)	pastry
pâte brisée	shortcrust pastry/dough used in quiche-bases
pâte de cassis	blackcurrant jellies
pâte de cédrat	citron fruit jellies
pâte feuilletée	crisp puff/flaky pastry
pâte filo	filo pastry
pâte frolle	almond pastry
pâte levée	yeast
pâte sablée	sweet crumbly pastry
pâte sucrée	french flan pastry
pâté	liver puree, often blended with other meats
pâté chaud de sole fécampoise	hot pâté of sole with oysters in pastry
pâté de campagne	a coarse textured liver mixture
pâté de fois	liver pâté
pâté de fois campagne	fine duck liver paste
pâté de fois gras	fine goose liver paste
pâté de fois gras en croûte	goose liver pâté in a raised pie of pastry
pâté de fois gras truffé	goose liver pâté
pâté du limousin	pork pie baked in brioche
pâté en croûte	pâté in a pastry crust
pâté lorrain	small pork pâtés in feuilleté
pâté maison	smooth minced and pounded liver mixture
patelle	limpet
pâtes (alimentaires)	pasta/noodles
pâtisseries	pastries
patisson	custard marrow
patranque	bread and cheese purée
pauie de mer	john dory (fish)
paupiettes	small rolled pieces/fillets of seasoned meat or fish (often stuffed)
pavé	i) usually rectangular shaped dessert or terrine ii) thick slice of beef steak
pavé de viande	thick piece of meat
pavots	poppy seeds
paysanne (à la)	cooked with small onions and diced bacon
pebronata	veal stew with red wine, pepper and tomato sauce
pêche	peach

peigne	scallop
pélardon	goat's milk cheese
pépins (sans)	pips/seeds (seedless)
pépites	nuggets
pepronata	veal/kid stew with red wine, pepper and tomato sauce
perche	perch
perche de mer	sea bass
perdreau	young partridge
perdrix	partridge
périgueux	i) a purée of goose or duck liver and truffles
	ii) truffle sauce
persil	parsley
persillade	chopped parsley often mixed with garlic
pet-de-nonne	small soufflé fritter/doughnut
pétéran	a mutton/veal and potato stew
pétillant	fully sparkling
petit déjeuner	breakfast
petit(e)	small
petite friture	deep fried little fish
petit gris	small snail
petit pain	bread roll
petit pain au cumin	bread roll with caraway seeds
petit pain au pavots	bread roll with poppy seeds
petits pains de foie	liver creams
petits pois	peas
petit suisse	pasteurised soft, unsalted cheese
pétoncle	queen scallop
pfutten	potato noodle squares
pibol(l)es	fried, tiny, young eels
picarde	onion sauce
pichet	jug
picholine	a large, long green variety of olive
plèce de boeuf	top of rump (beef)
pied de ...	head of (e.g. celery, asparagus, lettuce)
pied de boeuf	top rump (beef)
pied de mouton	mushroom
pieds de mouton	sheeps trotters
pieds de porc	pork trotters
pieds et paquets	mutton tripe cooked with sheep's trotters and vegetables

pieuvre	octopus
pigeon	pigeon
pigeonneau	squab
pignola	pine-nut cake
pignons	pine-nuts
pilaf	rice boiled in a bouillon with onions
pilau	pilaff (rice dish)
pilet	pintail duck
pilon	drumstick (poultry)
pil pil	cooked slowly
piment	sweet pepper/pimento(capsicum)
pimenté	hot/spicy
piment rouge	red pepper
piments	hot peppers
pince	claw (lobster/crab)
pincer	to sear food lightly
pinée	best quality dried cod
pintade	guinea fowl
pintadeau	young guinea cock
pipérade	a fluffy omelette with tomatoes, peppers, onion, garlic, garnished with slices of ham
piquant (e)	i) sharp/strong taste - sour (wine)
	ii) a thick slightly piquant white wine sauce with vinegar, shallots, capers, gherkins and tarragon
piqué	larded
piqué à l'ail	studded with garlic
piquenchagne	walnut and pear pie
pirot	sautéed goat with green garlic and sorrel
pissala	anchovy-flavoured essence
pissaladière	anchovies (or tiny fish), olive, onion and tomato tart or pizza - originating from nice
pissenlit	dandelion
pistache	i) mutton stew with beans, tomatoes and garlic
	ii) pistachio nut
pistils d'or	plum
pistou	i) a basil, parmesan and garlic sauce
	ii) provençal vegetable (often tomato) soup with garlic and basil
plaque de chocolat	bar of chocolate
plat-de-côte	flank (beef/pork) (shank - USA)
plat du jour	dish of the day

plateau de fromages	cheese board
platée	dish (ful), plate (ful)
plats de viande	meat dishes
plats végétariens	vegetarian dishes
pleurote	highly esteemed oyster mushroom
plie (franche)	plaice
plombières	tutti-frutti (ice cream)
pluvier en salmis	plover stew
poché (dans un liquide acidulé)	poached (soused)
pocheteau (blanc)	skate
pochouse	fish stew, most often eel, burbot, bream, cooked in wine and garlic - a burgundy speciality
poëlé	sautéed in hot frying pan
poëlé(e)	pot roasted on a bed of vegetables
poêlée	small fish dipped in flour and shallow fried
pognes aux confitures	sweet buns with jam
point (à)	i) medium cooked (steak)
	ii) ripe (cheese)
pointe de culotte	top rump (beef)
pointes d'asperges	asparagus tips
poirat	walnut and pear pie
poire	pear
poire belle angevine	a pear in liquer-syrup stuffed with ice cream
poire belle hélène	pear with vanilla ice cream and chocolate sauce
poire williams	pear distilled brandy
poireaux	leeks
pois cassés	split pea
pois chiches	chick peas
pois chiche grille	toasted chick-pea
pols chiches au gras	chick pea and sausage casserole
pois chinois	soya shoots
pois mange-tout	string peas/sugar snaps
poisson	fish
poisson pilote	pilot fish
poitrine (de boeuf)	brisket (of beef)
poivrade	pepper sauce with redcurrant jelly and cream
poivrade (à la)	espagnole sauce combined with stock and peppercorns
poivre	pepper
poivre (au)	served in black peppercorns

poivre blanc	white pepper
poivre de guinee	cayenne pepper/chilli pepper
poivre de la jamaïque	allspice
poivre en grains	whole peppercorns
poivre gris/noir	black pepper
poivre moulu/en poudre	ground pepper
poivre vert	green peppercorns
poivron (rouge/vert)	red/green sweet pepper
polenta	italian dish made of maize or cornflour
polonaise	a garnish of chopped hard-boiled eggs, capers and fried bread-crumbs, classically served with cauliflower/asparagus
polonaise (à la)	main ingredient stuffed and poached in red wine with almonds
pommade	thick, smooth paste
pomme	apple
pomme bonne-femme	baked apple
pomme cuites au four	baked apple
pomme (de) reinette	cox's orange pippin
pomme enrobé	apple dumplings baked or boiled
pommée bretonne	baked apples in batter with crushed macaroons
pommes (de terre)	potatoes
" **à la lyonnaise**	fried onions added to sauté potatoes
" **à la normande**	sliced potatoes, layered and baked with milk
" **alumettes**	"matchstick" potatoes
" **anna**	thinly sliced potatoes fried and baked
" **bigoudin**	crusty potato cake
" **boulangère**	thinly sliced potatoes and onions baked in dripping or stock
" **brayaude**	baked potatoes
" **château**	potatoes shaped like olives or baby potatoes cooked in butter
" **croquettes**	mashed potatoes in butter, rolled into small rounds, covered in breadcrumbs and deep-fried
" **darphin**	flat cakes of grated potatoes
" **dauphine**	mashed potatoes with butter and egg yolks/mixed in seasoned flour and deep fried
" **duchesse**	piped mashed potato made with butter and egg yolks
" **en robe des champs**	jacket potatoes
" **fermière**	stuffed baked potatoes

pommes (de terre)		potatoes
"	**fondantes**	potatoes cut into egg size and sautéed
"	**frites**	chips/french fries
"	**frites paille**	deep fried straw potatoes
"	**frits chatouillard**	fried ribbon potatoes
"	**gaufette**	lattice potato chips
"	**jacqueline**	sliced potatoes, coated with fromage blanc, and baked in small moulds
"	**maire**	sliced potatoes with cream
"	**mousseline**	mashed potatoes
"	**nature (au naturel)**	boiled/steamed potatoes
"	**nouvelles**	new potatoes
"	**paillasson**	flat potato cake
"	**sarladaises**	fried layers of thinly sliced potatoes and chopped truffles
"	**savoyarde**	sliced, layered potatoes baked with garlic and cheese
"	**toupinel**	hollowed-out baked potato mixed with egg, cream and cheese and re-baked in potato shell
"	**vapeur**	steamed/boiled potatoes

pommes au gratin — apple crumble
pommes bonne-femme — baked apples
pompe aux pommes — apple pie/large apple turnover
pompettes — orange flavoured brioche pastries
porcelet — piglet/sucking pig
porc frais à la basquaise — pork loin braised In milk
porché de bol — stew of pig's ears and feet
porquerolles — sea bass with herb stuffing
porto — i) port
ii) sauce with a port wine base
portugaise (à la) — garnish of tomatoes, shallots and mushrooms (sometimes pepper, herbs, courgettes and rice)
potage — soup
potage à l'ail — garlic soup
potage au cresson — watercress soup
potage aux noques — dumpling soup
potage bressane — pumpkin soup
potage gentilhomme — game and lentil soup
potage georgette — (globe) artichoke soup
potage saint germain — purée of split pea soup

potage/soupe bonne-femme	potato and leek soup, sometimes with carrots and occasionally bacon
pot-au-crème	creamy cold dessert of egg yolks, flavoured with vanilla/chocolate or coffee
pot-au-feu	stockpot/stew of boiled beef with vegetables
potée	casseroled pork-meat with cabbage, potatoes, carrots, sausage and herbs, often served as a substantial soup
potée auverginate	boiled pork with stuffed cabbage
potée lorraine	a thick pork, ham sausage and vegetable soup
potiron	pumpkin
pot je vleese, terrine flamande	rabbit, veal and pork terrine
pots de crème	chilled baked custards served in ramekin dishes (of various flavours)
pouce-pied	shellfish
pouding	pudding
pouillard	young partridge/pheasant
poularde	fattened pullet
poularde à la rennaise	stuffed chicken with prunes
poularde demi-devil	"chicken in half mourning" - a classic dish with chicken and thin slices of truffles poached gently and served with sauce suprême
poule	stewing fowl
poule au pot	casseroled/stewed chicken with vegetables
poulet	chicken
poulet basquaise	chicken with peppers
poulet en barbouille du berry	chicken with bacon in red wine and blood sauce
poulet fermièr	free-range chicken
poulet fermièr de grain	corn-fed chicken
poulet marengo	sautéed chicken served with garlic, mushrooms and tomato and truffle sauce. Usually accompanied with fried eggs and croutons
poulette	a velouté sauce with lemon and parsley, often used for sweetbreads
poulpe	octopus
poulpe à la marseillaise	casseroled octopus/in rice
pounti	ham and swiss chard flan
poupart	large crab

poupeton	i) meat roll (usually braised)
	ii) paté (usually fish) with cream and cheese
pour deux personnes	for two people
pourpier	purslane
pousse café	small spirit taken after coffee
poussin	spring chicken
poutargue	grey mullet roe with onions and hard-boiled eggs
praire	warty venus clam-eaten raw
praline	burnt almond
pralines d'aiguepeise	praline candies
pratelle	horse mushroom
précuit	precooked
premiers crus	prestigious wine
préparations	preparations
prépon	sweet melon
pré-salé	salt meadow sheep/lamb
pressé	squeezed
presse (à la)	pressed, squeezed
pression	draught (lager)
prévat	variety of mushroom
printanier	with spring vegetables
profiterole	a pastry puff filled with whipped cream or custard
provençale	a sauce consisting of onions, tomatoes and garlic
provençale (à la)	provençal dish generally indicating garlic/onion and olive oil often olives, tomatoes and aubergines are added
prune	plum/brandy
prune de damas	damson
pruneau(x)	prune
prunelle	sloe
psàlliote	horse mushroom (whitish and firm)
purée de ciboure	potato, dried bean and olive soup
purée vendéenne	cream of broad bean soup

Q

quartier	quarter/piece/portion
quasi	chump, thick part of loin (veal)

quatre épices	mixture of 4 ground spices - white pepper, cloves, nutmeg and ginger
quatre mendiants	mixed figs/almonds/raisins and hazelnuts
quatre quarts	pound cake
quenelles	light dumplings served with a velvety sauce (fish / poultry or meat)
quenelles de brochet	sausage-shaped pike - dumplings (steamed)
quetsche	plum-distilled brandy
quetsches	plums
queue	tail (fish dishes)
queue de boeuf	oxtail
quiche	a shell of unsweetened pastry filled with egg custard and a variety of fillings, cheese, vegetables etc.
quiche du mont d'or	light cream/roquefort cheese and egg filling
quiche lorraine	cheese and bacon flan

R

râble	saddle (hare/rabbit)
râble de lièvre à la cauchoise	saddle of hare with cream sauce
rabotte	apple dumpling
racine	root/root vegetable
raclette	melted cheese eaten with boiled potatoes, gherkins and pearl onions
radis	radishes
radis noir	horseradish
ragoût	hot pot/meat stew in a light gravy with vegetables
ragoût de boeuf	beef stew (rump, shoulder or rib cuts are used)
ragoût de cabillaud au safran	cod poached in onions, white wine and stock served in a tomato/cream and saffron stew
raie	skate
raie bouclée	thorn-backed ray
raifort	horseradish
raiponce	rampion
raisin	grape

raisin blanc/noir/vert	grape (white/black/green)
raisins de corinthe	currants (dried)
raisins de smyrne	sultana
raisins sec	raisins
raiteau/raiton	small skate
raito/raita	red wine sauce with garlic, herbs, capers and olives
ramequin	small tartlets or fondues with cheese
ramereau	young wood pigeon
ramier	wood pigeon
rapée morvandelle	grated potato and cheese cake
rascasse	fish used in bouillabaisse (usually scorpion or hog fish)
rastegais	fish cake
ratafia	i) small macaroon
	ii) liquer brandy with nutty or fruity flavour
ratatouille	provençal speciality - casserole of tomatoes /aubergine, onions, peppers and courgettes/garlic
rave	turnip
ravier	a small dish specifically used for the serving of hors d'oeuvre
ravigote	i) chopped tarragon, watercress, chives mixed with mustard and wine vinegar
	ii) spicy vinaigrette with mustard, gherkins and capers
rayon (de miel)	honeycomb
réglisse (bâtonde)	liquorice (stick)
reine-claude	greengage
reine des abeilles	a provençal cake of honey and chocolate
reinette	pippin apple
reinette grise	russet apple
relevée	raised
rémoulade	a mayonnaise sauce flavoured with mustard and herbs, capers, gherkins and anchovy fillets
renversée	inverted/mould
revenir	to "sear" food
rhubarbe	rhubarb
rhum	rum
rigodon	an ardeche speciality - sweet custard, served with walnuts/topped with blackcurrant jam
rigodon bourguignon	ham flan

rillettes de porc	chilled minced pork cooked in its own fat and served in earthenware pots
rippele	pork chop in red wine sauce
ris	sweetbreads (calf/lamb)
ris d'agneau	lamb sweetbreads
ris de veau	veal sweetbreads
rissolé	browned/fried
rissoler	to "sear" food
riz	rice
riz à la bayonnaise	rice with ham and baked eggs
robert	a brown mustard sauce with onions
rocambole	variety of shallot
rognonnade (de veau)	saddle of veal (with kidneys)
rognons	kidneys
rognons blanc	testicles, fried or poached and served with vinaigrette
romarin	rosemary
romsteck	beef steak taken from the top or lower part of sirloin
ronce-framboise	loganberry
ronde (de)	round/ring/plateful of ...
rondelle	slice (of sausage)
roquette	rocket (salad)
rosace	rose-shaped
rosbif	roast beef
rosé	rosé/pink
rosette	fillet
rosette de lyon	broad type of salami
rosoir	razor shell
rôti	roast
rôtie	herb-roasted slices of bread
rouelle	round slice
rouge	red
rougeot	smoked wild duck fillet
rouget (de roche)	red mullet (often not gutted)
rouille	a fiery, tomato-coloured, hot pepper and garlic mayonnaise
roulade (de boeuf)	rolled piece of meat (beef)
rouleau	roll
rouleau de printemps	spring roll
rousselet	variety of pear

roussette	dog fish/rock salmon
roussir	to brown (meat)
royale	with champagne
rue	rue
rumsteck	rump steak
russe (à la)	sour cream main feature of dish
russule	variety of mushroom
rutabaga	swede

S

sabayon	i) a creamy sauce served with dessert consisting of cream, eggs, sugar, white wine
	ii) a savoury sauce
sabayon de poisson	creamy fish mousse
sablé	shortbread biscuit
sablé(e) biquette	goat-cheese biscuit
sablés de bourg-dun	butter biscuits
sabre	scabbard fish
safran	saffron
sagou	sago
saignant	underdone /rare (steak)
saindoux	lard
saison (en)	in season
salade	salad
salade barcelone	tomatoes, green pepper, chicory salad with hard boiled eggs
salade bergerette	rice salad with eggs, cream (mustard optional)
salade cauchoise	potato salad with ham
salade cévenole	a salad consisting of cold duck confit, red cabbage, chestnuts and watercress
salade des moines	rice salad with asparagus and julienne strips of chicken - served with dressing
salade de thon	tuna salad
salade en chaponnade	mixed green salad with herbs and dressing, served with garlic croûtons

salade italienne	a mixed salad of vegetables, salami, anchovies, tomatoes, capers and olives (often covered in mayonnaise)
salade landaise	duck breast and mushroom (cèpe) salad
salade margot	a salad of celery, truffles, banana, curry flavoured dressing
salade mariette	salad of cooked shredded carrots, oranges and french dressing
salade mêlee	mixed salad
salade méli-mélo	mixed seasonal salad
salade normande	a rice and apple salad tossed in creamy dressing
salade provençale	fried tomatoes and aubergine cooked and mixed with anchovy fillets and rice. Tossed in dressing
salade russe	diced vegetable salad
salade verte	green salad
salade niçoise	a riviera dish of tossed green salad of tomatoes, potatoes, green beans, peppers, tuna fish, fennel, hard boiled eggs, anchovies and black olives
salé	salty
salmis (en)	stew
salpicon	i) minced/small regular dice of game/meat, mushrooms used for rissoles etc.
	ii) fillings for bouchée, patty cases etc.
salsifis	salsify/oyster plant
sancerre	light dry white wine
sandre	pike perch
sanglier	mature wild boar
sanguine	blood orange
sapin	fir tree (flavouring)
sapindor	green liquer made from fir cones
sarcelle	teal (small wild duck)
sardines	sardines
sarrasin	buckwheat flour
sarriette	savory
sarriette-commune	wild basil
sartagnado	small fish dipped in flour and shallow fried close together, resulting in a fish cake
sauce à la mie de pain	bread sauce
sàuce aigre-douce	sweet and sour sauce
sauce au safran	delicate fish sauce, flavoured with saffron

sauce aux briques	a sausage, black pudding and confit stew (cooked with garlic, tomatoes, peppers and herbs)
sauce aux poivrons rouge	a fish sauce with red peppers/garlic and onions
saucisses	sausages
saucisson	cold pork sausage
saucisson d'arles provençal	tomatoes grilled with oil, garlic and parsley
saucisson de lyon	dried ham/pork sausage, eaten raw
saucisson de ménage	home-made dried pork sausage, eaten as hors d'oeuvre
saucisson de montagne	dried pork sausage, eaten cold
saucisson de paris	large, short pork sausage
sauge	sage
saulpiquet	a ham dish with a spiced cream sauce
saumon	salmon
saumonette	dog fish
saupe	sea bream
saupiquet	i) piquant red wine and vinegar sauce
	ii) sautéed ham in cream sauce
sauté(e)	sautéed - food shaken in a little fat while frying
sauté de poulet à l'angevine	sauté of chicken with mushrooms and onions
sauterelle	shrimp
sauterne	a french white wine, much used in cookery
sauvage	wild/uncultivated
savarin	fondant cake/light pudding made from a yeast mixture
saveurs	flavours
savoyard (e)	dish cooked with cheese (usually gruyère)
scampi	prawns
scare	parrot fish
schifela	shoulder of pork with turnips
schweppes	tonic water
scipion	provençal name for very small cuttlefish
scorpène	scorpion fish
scorzonère	salsify
sec	straight/neat
seiche	cuttlefish
sel	salt
sel gemme	rock salt
selle	saddle

selon arrivage	when available
senteurs	perfume
serpolet	wild thyme
servi avec garniture	served with vegetables
service compris	service included
serviette	i) napkin
	ii) dish served in a "napkin", eg rice, jacket potato
sésames	sesame seeds
sherry	sherry
sirop des îles	caribbean syrup - a marinaded syrup of orange/lemons, vanilla, nutmegs and coriander
six-yeux	shellfish (ear-shaped)
socca	i) chick pea flour crêpes
	ii) polenta made from chick pea flour
sole	sole
sole mado	baked sole in cream sauce
solognote (à la)	stuffed and roasted with onion and tomato sauce
sorbet	a fruit or liqueur flavoured water ice
sorbier	sorb apple (similar to rowan)
sou fassum	stuffed cabbage
soubise	i) onion-cream sauce
	ii) onions used in cooking of dish
soufflé	i) a light, puffy dish based on egg whites and lightly flavoured with seafood, cheese or vegetables
	ii) a light gelatine - set sweet or savoury cream (similar to mousse)
soufflé au grand marnier	orange liqueur soufflé
soup au pistou	provençal speciality - vegetable soup with flavours of garlic, basil and olive oil (pesto)
soup d'étrilles	crab soup
soupe à l'ail	garlic soup
soupe à l'oignon	onion soup
soupe aux choux	cabbage soup
soupe bonne-femme	potato and leek soup, occasionally with bacon and/or carrots
soupe des pecheurs	fisherman's soup
soupe du berger	onion soup with cheese, tomatoes, leeks and garlic
soupe du jour	soup of the day

soupe normande	potato and cabbage soup
soupe solognote au lapin	rabbit and mushroom soup
sous-noix	topside (of meat)
specialités locales	local specialities
spécul(o)os	i) ginger biscuit (belgium)
	ii) spiced bun (belgium)
st. pierre	john dory (fish)
steack/steak	beef steak
steack tartare	raw minced beef served with raw egg yolk on top
sucre	sugar
sucré	sweet
sucre d'orge	barley sugar
sucrin	sweet melon
suer	to "sweat" food lightly
supions frits	deep fried small squid
supplément/en sus	extra charge
supplément pour changement de garniture	
	extra charge for alternative vegetable accompaniment
suprême	i) the wing and breast fillet removed in one piece from each side of a chicken carcass
	ii) a thickened velouté sauce with mushrooms and cream
suprême de volaille	chicken breast
sur commande	made to order
sureau	elderflower

T

table d'hôte	a general title - a meal of several courses at a fixed price
tajine (tagine)	i) earthenware cooking pot
	ii) meat or vegetable stew
talibars	pear dumplings
talmouses	puff pastry and almonds
tamarin	tamarind
tanche	tench (fish)

tapenade	a mediterranean sauce (used as a dip) consisting of anchovies, garlic, olives and capers
tapéno	capers
tarama	taramasalata
tartare	a mayonnaise flavoured with mustard and herbs or chopped gherkins/capers
tarte au fromage	cheese tart
tarte au moutarde	quiche with cheese and mustard filling
tarte aux pommes	apple pie/tart
tarte aux pommes grillagée	latticed apple tart
tarte des demoiselles tatin	caramelized apple or peach tart
tarte tartin	apple tart with shortcrust pastry
tartelette	small tart
tartelettes	round, golden shortcrust pastry cases
tartine	slice of bread and butter
tassergal	blue fish
taupe	shark
tautènes farcies	squid stuffed with onions and tomatoes, served au gratin with spinach
tende de tranche	silverside of beef
tendreté	tenderness (meat)
terrinée	baked rice pudding
terrine	similar to pâté, perhaps a little heavier or courser, served sliced from its terrine - resembles meat loaf and may consist of any meat, including game or fowl
têté de veau	veal's head
thé	tea
thé glacé	iced tea
thé vert (de chine)	china tea
thon	tuna
thym	thyme
tian	small earthenware dish
tiède	warm
tilleul	lime tree (flowers are used)
timbale	i) a thimble-shaped (not sized) mould ii) crusted hash, baked in a mould
tisane	herb tea
tisane d'orge	barley water
tomates	tomatoes

tombe	gurnard (fish)
topinambour	jerusalem artichoke
torchon	i) napkin, cloth
	ii) served in a "napkin" eg. jacket-potatoes, rice, truffles
totelots	hot noodle salad
tourangelle	salad of four or five vegetables, cooked and uncooked each with different dressing (artichokes, asparagus and green beans often used)
tourin	an aquitaine speciality - onion soup
tournedos	thick round slice of fillet steak
tourons	type of petits fours
tourte	i) layer cake
	ii) pie or tart (usually covered and savoury)
	iii) meat pie consisting of veal/pork/bacon and ham
tourte charollaise	open pear tart covered with cream
tourte de saumon	salmon feuilleté
tourte de viandes chaude	hot meat pasty
tourtière	i) pie dish/flan case
	ii) meat pie
tourtisseaux	yeast fritters, flavoured with orange-flower water
tourton	thick pancake made with buckwheat flour
toute épice	all spice
train	hind quarters
train de côtes	rib (of beef)
tranche	slice/steak
tranche napolitaine	slice of neapolitan ice-cream
tranches de fruits glacées	glazed fruits
tresse	plait/braid
trevise	red chicory (salad)
tripes	tripe
tripes à la mode de caen	tripe/calf's trotters baked with vegetables, apple brandy or cider
tripotcha	mutton blood sausage with red pepper and nutmeg
trompette de la mort	a trumpet-shaped edible fungus
tronçon	section/piece
trouchia	flat omelette with spinach and swiss chard

truffade	an auvergne speciality - potato cakes fried in rounds, with melted cheese and grilled
truffé	truffle (underground fungus)
truffiat	potato cake
truite (arc-en-ciel)	trout (rainbow)
truite au bleu	trout poached in court-bouillon (stock)
truite de rivière	river trout
truite farcie du périgord	trout stuffed with ham and cèpes (mushrooms)
truite meunière	well seasoned trout, fried in butter
truites à la mont bardoise	trout stuffed with spinach and shallots
truite saumonée	salmon trout
trumeau	leg/shin (beef)
ttoro	peppery onion and fish soup
tuile	almond slice
tuiles	wafers
tuiles aux amandes	small almond pastry baskets
turbotière	fish kettle
turbot vallée d'auge	turbot in cider and apple sauce
turinois	chocolate chestnut pudding

U

unchères	small lemon and vanilla tarts
une tasse de thé	cup of tea

V

vacherin glacé	ice cream cake/meringue and cream
vanette	queen scallop
vangeren	dace (river fish)
vanille	i) vanilla
	ii) a sweet vanilla-flavoured liquer
vanneau	queen scallop
vapeur	steam
varèche	seaweed/kelp
varié (e)	assorted

vaudoise	dace (small fish)
veau	veal
velouté	a glossy, velvety thickened chicken or meat stock
velouté de tomates	cream of tomato soup
velouté de volaille	cream of chicken soup
ventrèche	breast of pork (salted or smoked)
verdette	a variety of mushroom
vermicelle	very fine strings of wheat-flour pasta/vermicelli
vermouth	vermouth
vernon	(fish) coated in breadcrumbs and grilled, served with ravigote sauce
veronique	a sauce consisting of grapes and wine
verre	glass
verte	i) green ii) green mayonnaise with spinach/watercress and/or herbs
vert bonnet	a variety of mushroom
vesse de loup géante	puff-ball mushroom
vessie	pig's bladder
veulaise (à la)	dish with watercress sauce
viande	meat
viande de cheval	horsemeat
viande sans os	boned meat
viande séchée	cured dried beef
vichyssoise	potato and leek soup
vigneau	winkle
vigneron(ne) (à la)	dish cooked with grapes, wine, vine leaves and brandy or marc
vignette	winkle
vignot	winkle
vinaigre	vinegar
vinaigre d'alcool	distilled vinegar
vinaigrette	vinegar and white wine dressing
vinaigrette mimosa	french dressing mixed with processed hard boiled egg
vin(s)	wine(s)
vincent	green herb mayonnaise
vin chaud	mulled wine
vin du cru	local wine
vin ordinaire	table wine

vive	weever (sea fish)
vodka	vodka
voile de mariée	strudel type dough/filo pastry often substituted
voiture	trolley (of desserts)
volailles	poultry
vol-au-vent	light puff pastry with various fillings
volonté (à)	unlimited

W

waldorf	apple, celeriac,walnut salad
waterzooi de poissons	freshwater fish stew in butter sauce (cold/hot jellied sauce with gherkins and capers)

X

xérès	sherry

Y

yaourt/yoghourt	yoghurt
yogourt maison	homemade yoghurt

Z

zéphire	i) mould shaped ii) small oval-shaped forcemeat dumpling, poached and served with rich sauce
zeste	rind/peel (lemon/orange)

*The cheese course is generally
served before the dessert and
is rarely accompanied with a menu.
As there are many French cheeses,
which are not found in the British
Isles, the following section may help
for speed of reference, when
the cheese-board arrives*

Fresh cheeses   -are distinct from other
cheeses in not being
fermented

Fermented cheeses - made from raw curds are
of two kinds

* soft cheeses (e.g. brie, coulommiers
camembert.)

* hard cheeses (e.g. cantal, roquefort,
gorgonzola etc.)

There are also cheeses made from scalded curds
(e.g. gruyère, port-salut etc.)

Les fromages – cheeses

A

aisy cendrée   a soft cheese, made from cows' milk and dried under the ashes of vine wood

aunis   a ewes'-milk cheese, triangular in shape, - a charente-maritime speciality

B

banon   a small round goat cheese, wrapped in chestnut or other savoury leaves and passed through a bath of eau-de-vie or marc and then tied round with straw while being dried. A fairly strong but delicate flavour

barbery   soft, camembert-like cheese

beaufort   a rare cheese, similar in taste to gruyère, but perhaps a little fatter in flavour

beaujolais   small goat cheeses - a mâconnais speciality

beaupré de roybon   a similar cheese to reblochon - a cows' milk, yellow coloured cheese, which is round and thick in shape with a fairly soft texture. Its flavour resembles port salut

bleu d'auvergne   a blue cheese, similar to roquefort but made from cows'milk

bleu de l'aveyron   a blue-green veined cows' milk cheese

bleu de bresse   a blue-veined cheese, similar to gorgonzola but much softer and creamier

bleu des causses   a cows' milk cheese with a blue-green veined appearance

bleu de corse   a cheese similar to roquefort

bleu de haut jura   a large cheese, made from cows' milk with a blue green veined appearance

bleu de laqueuille   a blue-vein cheese made from cows' milk, similar taste to roquefort

bleu de quercy   a blue veined cows' milk cheese, similar to bleu d'aveyron

Les fromages – cheeses

bleu de thiesac	a blue cheese, similar to roquefort and made from cows'milk
bleu de vélay	a cows' milk cheese, blue veined and similar to roquefort
bossons macérés	a goats' milk cheese, mixed with olive oil, herbs, wine or brandy
bouillie	bland creamy mild cheese
bourgain	a fresh, soft light cheese
boutons de culotte	small goat cheese
brie	a soft delicately flavoured cheese, shouldn't be too runny
brique	square-shaped cows' and goats' milk cheese
briquebec	a mild cheese
brousses	a fresh, ewes' milk cheese

C

cabecou	a goats' milk cheese, small and flat
cabion	a square shaped cheese of mixed cows' and goats' milk
cabrion	a cows' milk cheese, wrapped in plane leaves
cachat	a strong cheese made from ewes' milk mixed with wine and brandy
caillebotte	a cheesey form of yogurt
camembert	pale lemon, soft, delicately-flavoured cheese
cancaillotte	a very strong cheese - made from skimmed cows' milk, with wine and/or brandy added
cantal	resembles a mature british cheese - made from cows' milk and shaped into cylinders
cantalon	a smaller version of a cantal cheese
carré de l'est	a square shaped, semi-hard cheese, best likened to a mild maroilles
chabichou	squat, cylindrically shaped cheese, made from goats' milk
chabris	a fairly firm, medium strength goats' cheese
chambaraud	similar to reblochon or port salut - a soft textured, round yellow cheese

Les fromages – cheeses

chaource   a small, creamy rich cheese
chef boutonne   a round or square goats' milk cheese
chèvrotins   small goat cheese
chèvrotin d'ambert a strong smelling and highly flavoured
                      goats or goat and cow milk cheese - small
                      and rectangular in shape
chèvrotin de mâcon small goat cheeses
chèvrotin de moulins a pyramid-shaped goat cheese, rather
                      strong in smell and flavour
citeaux   a cows' milk cheese
claqueret   a fresh soft cheese which is mixed with
                      chives and onions
comté   a cows' milk cheese, similar to swiss gruyère
                      but with very few holes
coulommiers   a type of brie (a cheaper version)
cremets   a small cream cheese, either goats or cows
                      and goats' milk mixed
cremets nantais   a summer cheese - small and fresh
croix d'or   a small goats' milk cheese
crottin de chavignol a tall, round but small goat cheese

E

époisses   a soft cheese made from cows' milk
ervy   a type of brie

F

fontainebleau   a very light cream cheese
fourme d'ambert   a type of cantal cheese but blue-veined
fourme de montbrison a blue veined cantal (similar to a mature
                      british cheese)
frinault affiné   a similar cheese to olivet
fromage à la pie   a cheaper version of brie

Les fromages – cheeses

fromage de banon   a flattish, small cheese made from goats' milk, usually wrapped in chestnut or other leaves

fromage de la tappe
** d'echourgnac**   a fresh cows' milk cheese

fromage des laumes   a dark brown coloured cheese - said to be the result of being washed in water containing coffee

fromage de tamié   a moderately soft cows' milk cheese

fromage de troyes   a soft camembert-like cheese

fromage du curé   a small square cheese, made from cows' milk

fromage fort   in appearance this looks like a mild cheese spread but it is a very strong cheese made from skimmed cows' milk

G

gaperon   a hard strong cheese, spherical in shape

géromé   occasionally flavoured with aniseed, fennel or cumin, an extremely strong ripe cheese. It is made from cows' milk and is round with an orangish crust

gex   a cows' milk cheese with blue-green veining

gien   a cheese made from a mixture of goat and cow milk - a squat cylindrical shape in appearance

H

hollande   a mild dutch cheese, similar to edam in taste and appearance

Les fromages – cheeses

J

jonchée   set in a rush container, either a cows' milk or goats' milk fresh cheese

L

laguiole   rather like a matured british cheese - made from cows' milk and shaped like a stocky cylinder - equivalent to cantal in taste

laruns   a ewes' milk cheese, cylindrically shaped and varying from moderately strong to creamier, depending on region

levroux   a pyramid shaped goats' cheese, fairly firm and medium strong

livarot   an extremely strong tasting cheese round and flat in appearance

lormes   a medium strong goats' milk cheese

lorraine   a large munster (cows' milk cheese with orangish rind and extremely strong taste)

M

macquelines   is a type of brie which is also reminiscent of camembert

mamirolle   an oblong shaped cows' milk cheese

maroilles   a deep yellow cheese with a very definite rich flavour, square in appearance with a brownish yellow rind

Les fromages – cheeses

mignot
a rather soft cheese, a choice between fresh (blanc) or ripened (passé) can be either round or square shaped. A cheese ripened for three months can be really strong in flavour

monsieur fromage
a mild, bland creamy cheese

mont cenis
usually a mixture of cow, ewe and goat milk, this is a hard cheese with a blue mould

mont d'or
a lyonnais cows' milk cheese

morbier
a round cows' milk cheese - black lines in the cheese denotes use of charcoal to rub edges when still in the mould

mothe saint héray
often dried between plane leaves, this cheese most resembles a small camembert

munster
a thick round cheese made from cows' milk. Not a hard cheese but when ripe is extremely strong tasting

murol
a type of saint nectaire, semi-hard cows' milk cheese with a distinctive hole in the middle

N

neufchâtel
when eaten young (fleuri) it is soft, mild and creamy, if left to mature (affiné) it becomes fairly strong tasting

O

olivet
made in a factory, it resembles coulommlers (a cheaper version of brie)

oloron
a fairly strong ewes' milk cheese

oustet
a cheese flavoured with sweet pepper

Les fromages – cheeses

P

persillé des aravis   a soft blue-green veined cheese made from goats' milk

petit pot de poitiers   a fresh cheese made from goats' milk

petit suisse   extremely delicate and creamy cheese often freshly made - small and round in appearance

picodon   a soft goat cheese

picotin de saint agrève   a round cheese, very similar to camembert

pithiviers au foin   a cheaper version of brie, its surface sprinkled with grain

poivre d'âne   a goat cheese or one of mixed goat and cow milk, its most often flavoured with savory and rosemary

pont l'éveque   a famous square cheese, semi-hard and fermented, salty and very strong

port salut   a creamy, yellow whole-milk cheese

pouligny saint pierre   a fairly firm and medium strong goat cheese

poustagnac   a fresh milk cheese, flavoured with sweet pepper

R

reblochon   a fairly soft textured cheese, a little like port salut. It is yellow, round and thick in appearance

rigotte   a cheese of mixed cow and goat milk, thin and round in shape

rigottes   small goat cheeses

rocamadour   a small goat cheese

roquefort   a ewes' milk cheese, blue veined, strong tasting and salty

ruffec   a thick cylindrical cows' milk cheese

Les fromages – cheeses

s

saint agathon	small, flat, round goat cheese
saint agur	a pasteurised cow's milk cheese, octagonal cylinder in shape, with a cream/yellow, blue grey mould appearance - a creamy texture and spicy blue-cheese taste
saint benoît	a cheese resembling olivet, a soft cheese often rubbed with salt
saint claude	served either as a fresh or mature cheese, made from goats' milk
saint florentin	a white fresh cheese made from cows' milk
saint loup	a goats' cheese, cylindrical in shape
saint marcellin	a soft and creamy cheese, round and flat in appearance
saint nectaire	a semi-hard cheese made from cows' milk
saint rémy	a very rich type of munster cheese
sainte marie	a white fresh cows' milk cheese
sainte maure	a small cylinder shaped goat cheese
sauzé	a cylindrical goat cheese
septimoncel	a mixture of cow and goat milk, with a blue green veined appearance

T

thénay	a soft, cows' milk cheese, very similar to camembert
thoissey	a cork shaped goats' milk cheese
tignard	a cows' milk cheese
tomme de brach	a ewes' milk cheese
tomme au fervouil	a ewes' milk cheese, fennel flavoured
tomme de savoie	a cows' milk cheese, round, tall and large in appearance
tournon saint martin	a flat round goats' cheese, a fairly firm and medium strong taste
trois cornes	a cows' milk cheese

Les fromages – cheeses

V

vachard
a cows' milk cheese, semi-hard with a yellowish-red crust

vacherin
a soft cows' milk cheese, may be found wrapped in pine or cherry bark

vacherin des bauges
a fairly soft cows' milk cheese. A round thickish shape - similar to coulommiers when ripe

valençay
a pyramid-shaped goat cheese, with a medium strong taste

vendôme
a factory-made cheese, similar to brie, it may be bleu or cendré

véritable nantais
a mild cows' milk cheese, small and square in appearance

vézelay
a small, goats' milk cheese

villiers
a factory-made cheese, very similar to coulommiers

ENGLISH TO FRENCH
SECTION

A

alcoholic drinks	boissons alcoolisées
alfafa sprouts	germes de luzerne
allspice	toute-épice
almond and cream tartlets	mirlitons
almond biscuit/cookie	friand sucré
almond pastry	pâte frolle/marcellin
almond slice	tuite
almonds	amandes
almonds blanched	amandes mondées
almonds roasted	amandes grillées
anchovy	anchois
angel fish	ange de mer
angelica	angélique
angler (fish)	baudroie
aniseed	anis
aniseed-based drink	pastis
apple	pomme
apple crumble	pommes au gratin
apple distilled brandy	calvados
apple juice	jus de pomme
apple-stuffed pastry	craquelin
apple tart (caramelised)	tarte des demoiselles tatin
apple tart (latticed)	tarte aux pommes grillagée
apple tart (pie)	tarte aux pommes
apple turnover	chausson aux pommes
apricot	abricot
apricot (halved)	oreillons
apricot and brandy liqueur	abricotine
apricot juice	nectar d'abricot
artichoke (globe)	artichaut
asparagus	asperges
asparagus tips	pointes d'asperges
assorted	varié(e)
aubergine	aubergine
avocado	avocat

B

bacon	lard/bacon
baked	(cuit) au four
baked (in greaseproof paper)	en chemise
baked alaska	omelette norvégienne
baked (steamed) pudding	soufflé
balm (lemon)	mélisse
banana	banane
banana liqueur	banadry
bar of chocolate	plaque de chocolat
barley	orge
barley corn	grain d'orge
barley sugar	sucre d'orge
barley water	tisane d'orge
barracuda	brochet de mer
basil	basilic
bass	bar
batter	pâte à frire
bay leaf	laurier
bean sprouts/shoots	germes de soja
beans - broad	fèves
beans - french	haricots verts
beans - haricot	haricots blancs
beans - runner	haricots d'espagne
beef	boeuf
beef steak	biftec
beer	bière
beetroot	betterave
belgian buns	spéculos
bell pepper/capsicum (red) (green)	piment (rouge) (vert)
best wine	premiers crus
bilberries	myrtilles
biscuit wafer	gaufre
biscuits	sablés
bitter	amer
blackberries	mûres
black cherry spirit	kirsch

blackcurrant drink	cassis
blackcurrants	cassis
blanched	mondée
blood orange	sanguine
blueberries	myrtilles
boar (wild)	sanglier
boar (young/wild)	marcassin
boiled	i) bouilli
	ii) cuit à l'eau/bouillie
boiled potatoes	pommes (de terre) nature
boned cutlets	noisettes
bonito	bonite (à dos rayé)
borage	bourrache
bottled	en bouteille
brains	cervelle
braised	braisé
braised (meat)	étuvée
brandy	i) armagnac
	ii) cognac
brandy (plum etc.)	eau-de-vie
brandy-snap	biscotte au gingembre
brazil nut	noix de brésil
bread (brown) (white)	
(wholemeal)	pain (bis) (blanc) (complet)
bread and butter (slice)	tartine
breadcrumbs	chapelure
bread fruit	fruit à pain
bread roll	petit pain
bread sauce	sauce à la mie de pain
bread stick	gressin
breakfast	petit déjeuner
bream (black)	dorade gris
bream (fresh water)	brème
bream (red)	dorade commune
bream (sea water)	griset/pagre commun
breast/wing fillet	suprême
brill	barbue
brioche ring (with	
saffron and anise)	bistorto
broad beans	fèves
broccoli	chou brocolis

browned/fried	rissolé
brussel sprouts	choux de bruxelles
bunting	ortolan
burbot	lotte
burgundy	bourgogne
butter	beurre
butter biscuits	sablés de bourg-dun

C

cabbage (red)	chou (rouge)
cabbage (spring)	chou de mai
cake	gâteau
calabrese	broccoli
calf	veau
capers	câpres
capon	chapon
capsicum/bell pepper	
(red) (green)	piment (rouge) (vert)
carafe	carafe
caramel pudding	crème caramel
caraway (seeds)	carvi (graines de)
cardamom	cardamome
cardoon	cardon
caribbean cabbage	caraïbe
carp	carpe
carrots	carottes
carrots (glazed)	carottes à la vichy
cashew nut	noix de cajou
cauliflower	chou-fleur
cayenne pepper	poivre de cayenne
celeriac	céleri rave
celery	céleri
celery stick	une côte de céleri
cereal	céréale
champagne	champagne
char (fish)	omble (chevalier)
chard	blette/bette

cheese	fromage
cheese (goats)	fromage chèvre (see cheese section)
cheese sauce	mornay
cheese tart	tarte au fromage
cheese topping	gratin
chef's recommendation	le chef vous propose
cherries (black)	cerises (noires)
cherry	griotte/guigne
cherry and custard tart	mias bourbonnais
cherry distilled brandy	kirsch
chervil	cerfeuil
chestnut (candied)	marron glacé
chestnut dessert (puréed)	mont-blanc
chestnuts	châtaignes/marrons
chick peas	pois chiches
chicken	poulet
chicken (breast)	suprême de volaille
chicken broth (thickened)	suprême
chicken (spring)	poussin
chickpea	chiche
chicory	endive (rouge) trevise/chicon/endive belges
chilli - (red) (green)	piment (rouge) (vert)
chilli pepper	poivre de guinee
china tea	thé vert (de chine)
chine/loin (usually pink)	échine
chinese leaves	chou de chine
chips	pommes (de terre) frites
chiterlings (sausage)	andouille(tte)
chives	ciboulette
chocolate	chocolat
chocolate (hot)	un chocolat (chaud)
chocolate cake	gâteau au chocolat
chocolate chestnut pudding	turinois
chocolate log	marquisette
chocolate pudding	mousse au chocolat
chocolate sponge cake	caraque
chopped small/fine	hacher menu
chops	côtelettes
choux pastry (pyramid)	croquembouches

chump, thick part of loin (usually veal)	quasi
cider	améléon
cinnamon	cannelle
cinnamon and apple pastry	choquart
citrus fruits	agrumes
clams	palourdes/clovisse/praire/coque/blanchet
claret (wine)	bordeaux (vin)
clove of garlic	gousse d'ail
cloves	clous de girofle
coated/topped	nappé de
coated/wrapped	fichie
cockle	coque
coconut	noix de coco
cod (dried)	morue
cod (fresh)	cabillaud
coffee	un café
coffee - black	café noir/nature
coffee-decaffinated	café décaféiné
coffee-espresso	café un express
coffee-finely ground	café moulu
coffee-sponge cake	moka
coffee/tea spoon	cuiller à café/à thé
coffee with cream	café crème
coffee with milk	café au lait
cognac fritters	merveilles charentaises
cold	froid(e)
combination/mixture of ...	méli-mélo
common/ordinary	ordinaire
conger eel	congre
conserve (goose)	confit
continental breakfast	café complet
cooked in wrapping (paper/foil)	(en) papillote
coriander	coriandre
cornet (ice cream)	cornet de glacé
cornflakes	flocons de maïs
cornmeal cakes (fried)	cruchades
cornmeal pudding with raisins	millasson
corn on the cob	papeton

cos lettuce	laitue romaine
courgette	courgette
crab	crabe
cracker biscuit	craquelïn/biscuit salé
cranberries	canneberges
cranberry	airelle/canneberge
crayfish	écrevisses
cream (double)	crème épaisse
cream (lightly whipped)	crème fleurette
cream (whipped)	crème fouettée
creamy	crémeux(euse)
crisp/crunchy	croquant
crisps	chips
crumb	miette
crunchy/crisp	croquant
crystallised (fruit)	confit
cucumber	concombre
cup	tasse
curd cheese	fromage blanc
currants (dried)	raisins de corinthe
curry sauce	indienne
curry/curry sauce	cari
custard	crème anglaise
custard (with caramel)	crème caramel
custard apple (fritters or poached)	anone
custard flan (baked)	flaugnard limousine
custard marrow	patisson
cutlet (veal)	côte (de veau)
cutlets - (scallop)	escalope
cuttle fish	scipion/seiche

D

damson	prune de damas
dandelion	pissenlit
dark (beers etc.)	brune
dates	dattes

deer (red)	cerf
desserts	desserts
devilled eggs	oeufs à la diable
dill	aneth
dish of the day	plat du jour
double cream	crème épaisse
doughnut (warm)	beignet (soufflé)
draught (lager)	pression
dried fruit	fruits secs
drink included	boisson comprise
drinks	boissons
dry (very)	sec (brut)
dublin bay prawns	langoustines
duck (wild)	canard (sauvage)
duckling	caneton
dumplings	quenelles
dumplings (pear)	talibars

E

eel	anguille
egg and wine custard	crème bachique
egg plant/aubergine	aubergine
eggs	oeufs
eggs - fried	oeufs poêlés
eggs - poached	oeufs pochés
eggs - scrambled	oeufs brouillés
eggs - soft boiled	oeufs à la coque
endive	chicorée/frisée
espresso coffee	express
extra charge	supplément/en sus

F

fat	gras
fennel	fenouil
fenugreek	fenugrec
field bean	féverole
figs	figues
fillet steak	filet
first course	entrées
fish	poisson
fish kettle	turbotière
fish steak	darne
fish stew	bourride
fizzy	gaseux
flaky pastry	pâte feuilletée
flap mushrooms	cèpes
flounder	flétan
flour	farine
fondant cake	savarin
food	nourriture
foreign (drinks etc.)	étrangère
fork	fourchette
fowl	volaille
fowl (stewing)	poule
free range chicken	poulet fermièr
french beans	haricots verts
french fries	pommes (de terre) frites
fresh	frais
fried	frit
fritter	beignet
frogs' legs	cuisses de grenouilles
fruit juice	jus de fruits
fruit salad	fruits rafraîchis/macédoine de fruits
full bodied	corsé

G

game	gibier
garlic	ail
garlic soup	aïgo bouïdo
garnish	garniture
gateau	gâteau
gherkins	cornichons
gin and tonic	gin - tonic
ginger	gingembre
gingerbread	pain d'épices
glass	verre
glazed	glacé
globe artichoke	artichaut
goat	chèvre (f) bouc(m)
goat (kid)	cabri
goose	oie
gooseberries	groseilles à maquereaux
grape (green/black)	raisin (blanc/noir)
grape distilled brandy	marc
grapefruit	pamplemousse
grapefruit juice	jus de pamplemousse
greengage	reine-claude
green leaves	feuilles vertes
green salad	salade verte
grilled	grillé
grilled meat	grillades
grinder (coffee/pepper)	moulin (à café/poivre)
guava	goyave
gudgeon	goujons
guinea cock (young)	pintadeau
guinea fowl	pintade
gurnet	grondin

H

haddock	aiglefin/aigrefin
hake	merlu/colin
hake (dried)	merluche
hake (raw)	ceviche
half	demi
half bottle	demi-bouteille
halibut	flétan
ham	jambon (de bayonne)
hard boiled	dur
hare (wild)	lièvre
haricot beans	haricots blancs
hazelnut	noisette
herbs (cooked with)	fines herbes
herb tea	tisane
herring	hareng
herring roe	laitance
home-made	(fait à la) maison
honey	miel
honey cakes	nonnettes
honeycomb	rayon de miel
horseradish	raifort/radis noir
hot	chaud(e)
hot chocolate	chocolat chaud
hot (spicy)	pimenté
hyssop	hysope

I

ice cream	glace
ice cream cake	vacherin glace
ice cream cornet	cornet de glace
iced	glacé
iced tea	thé glacé

J

jacket potatoes	pommes (de terre) en rope des champs
jam	confiture
jellied	en gelée
jelly	gelée
jerusalem artichoke	topinambour
john dory	st. pierre/dorée/jean doré/pauie de mer
jugged (hare)	civet (de lièvre)
juice	jus
juniper berries	genièvre

K

kale	chou frisé
kebab	brochette
kid goat	cabri
kidney beans	flageolets
kidneys	rognons
kiwi	kiwi
knife (and fork)	couteau (couvert)
knuckle	jarret
kohlrabi	chou rave

L

ladies fingers/okra	gombaut/gombos
lake salmon	féra
lamb	agneau
lamprey	lamproie
large	grand(e)
lark	alouette
layer cake	tourte

lean/thin meat	maigre
leeks	poireaux
leg (of lamb)	gigot
lemon	citron
lemonade	limonade
lemon and strawberry ice cream (in kirsch)	coupe jacques
lemon curd	crème de citron
lemon grass	citronelle
lemon ice	colonel
lemon jelly with grapes and cream	chartreuse au citron
lemon juice	citron pressé
lentils(yellow)	lentilles (jaunes)
lettuce	laitue
lettuce-lambs	mâche
lettuce-red oak leaf	feuille de chêne
lichee/lychee	letchi/litchi
light (beer etc.)	blonde
light (taste)	léger
light dry white wine	i) alsatian
	ii) muscadet
lightly salted	demi-sel
lime	limon
limpet	patelle
liquor	liquer
liquorice	réglisse (bâtonde)
liver	foie
liver pâté	pâté de fois
lobster (spiny)	homard (langoste)
local specialities	specialités locales
local wine	vin du cru
loganberry	ronce-framboise
loin/chine (usually pink)	échine
loin strip steak	contre filet
lovage	livèche
lump fish	lompe
lunch	déjeuner

M

macaroni	milanaise
mace	macis
mackerel	maquereau
madeira wine	madère
mango	mangue
marinaded	mariné
marjoram	marjolaine
marmalade	confiture d'oranges
marrow	courge/moelle
marzipan	massepain
mashed potatoes	pommes (de terre) mousseline
mayonnaise (garlic)	aïoli
meat	viande
meatballs	boulettes
medium (cooked)	à point
medium ripe (cheese)	à point
melba toast	biscotte
melon	melon/charentais/canteloup
meringues (with cream)	baiser
mild ale	bière brune
milk	lait
milk-cold	lait froid
milk-hot	lait chaud
milkshake	frappé
mince (meat)	haché
mineral water	l'eau minérale
mineral water (fizzy)	l'eau gazeuse
mineral water (still)	l'eau non gazeuse
mint	menthe
mixed	panache
mixed vegetables	macédoine de legumes
mixture/combination of ...	méli-mélo
mixture of herbs	fines herbes
molasses/treacle	mélasse
monkfish	gigot de mer/baudroie lotte-de mer
morels	morilles
mulberries	mûres
mung beans	haricot mung

mushrooms	champignons (de paris)
mushrooms-boletus	bolets
mushrooms-caesars	oronge
mushrooms (cooked with)	forestière
mushrooms-flap	cèpes, chanterelle, girolle
mushrooms-parasol	grisotte
mushrooms-wild	fruits des bois
mussels	moules
mustard	moutarde
mutton	mouton
myrtle	myrte

N

napkin	serviette
nasturtium	capucine
natural	naturelle
neck	cou
nectarine	brugnon
nettles	orties
new potatoes	pommes (de terre) nouvelles
non-alcoholic drinks	boissons sans alcoolisées
noodles	nouilles
nutmeg	noix (de) muscade/muscade

O

oak-leaf lettuce	feuille de chêne
oat cakes	galette d'avoine
oatmeal	farine d'avoine
octopus	poulpes
offal	abats
oil	huile
okra/ladies fingers	gombos/gombaut

omelette	omelet(te)
onion/cream sauce	soubise
onions	oignons
onions (cooked with)	lyonnaise
orange	orange
orangeade	orangeade
orange biscuits (crisp)	caladons
orange cake	gateau sévillan
orange juice	jus d'orange
ordinary/common	ordinaire
oregano	origan
ortolan bunting	ortolan
oyster plant/salsify	salsifis
oysters	huîtres

P

pancake (sweet)	crêpe (falue)
papawa/papaya	papaye
parsley	persil
parsnip	panais
partridge	perdrix
partridge young	perdreau
passion-fruit	barbadine
pasta	pâtes
pastries	pâtisseries
pastry	pâte
paw-paw	papaye
peach	pêche
peanuts	cacahouètes/cacahuetes
pear	poire
pear brandy	poire williams
pear with vanilla ice cream	poire belle hélène
pearl barley	orge perlé
peas	petits pois
peas-split	pois cassés
peas-string	pois mange-tout
peel/rind	zeste

pepper (white) (black)	poivre (blanc) (gris/noir)
pepper (ground)	poivre moulu/en poudre
pepper/capsicum (red) (green)	piment (rouge) (vert)
peppermint	menthe anglaise, poivrée
pepper sauce	poivrade
peppers (sweet)	poivrons
perch	perche
pernod	pernod
pheasant	faisan
pickled	confit au vinaigre
pie crust	chapeau
pie/tart	tourte
piece/portion	quartier
pigeon	pigeon
pig's knuckle	jambonneau
pike	brochet
pilot fish	fanfre
pimiento	piment
pineapple	ananas
pine nuts	pignons
pine-nut cake	pignola
pink/rosy	rosé
pistachio	pistache
pistachio-flavoured cake	galicien
plaice	plie/carrelet
plain	naturelle/nature
plate (soup)	assiette (creuse)
plum-distilled brandy	quetsche
plum tart	anglois
plums	prunes
poached	poché
pollack (fish)	lieu
pomegranate	grenade
poppy seeds	pavots
pork	porc
pork pie	pâté de porc (en croûte)
port	porto
porterhouse steak	chateaubriand
potato cake (flat)	pommes de terre paillasson
potatoes	pommes (de terre)

potatoes boiled	pommes (de terre) nature
potato chips	pommes (de terre) frites
potatoes (cooked with)	parmentier
potato crisps	chips
potatoes-jacket	pommes (de terre) en robe des champs
potatoes-mashed	pommes (de terre) duchesse
potatoes mashed and deep fried	pommes (de terre) dauphine
potatoes-matchstick	pommes (de terre) alumettes
potatoes-new	pommes (de terre) nouvelles
potatoes-steamed	pommes (de terre) vapeur
poultry	volailles
praline candies	pralines d'aigue peise
prawns (large)	scampi (gambas)
pre-cooked	précuit
prickly pear	figue de barbarie
prunes	pruneaux
pudding	pouding
puff pastry cone	cannelon
puff pastry (fine layers)	mille feuilles
pullet (fatted)	poularde
pumpkin	potiron
purslane	pourpier

Q

quail	caille
quarter piece/portion	quartier
queen scallop	vanneau/vanette
quince	coing

R

rabbit	lapin
rack of lamb	carré d'agneau
radishes	radis
raisins	raisins secs
rare (underdone)	saignant
rare (very)	bleu
rascasse	fish/bouillabaisse
raspberries	framboises
raw/uncooked	cru
raw vegetable starter	crudités
red	rouge
red pepper	piment rouge
redcurrants	groseilles
red deer	cerf
red mullet	rouget/barbet
red pepper/capsicum	piment rouge
rhubarb	rhubarbe
rib	côte
rib chop (beef)	côte (de boeuf)
rib eye steak	entrecôte
rice	riz
rind/peel	zeste
ring biscuit	gimblette
ripe	affiné
river trout	truite de rivière
roast	rôti
roast beef	rosbif
rock partridge	bartavelle
rocket (salad)	roquette
rocks (on the)	avec des glaçons
roe deer	chevreuil
roll-mop	hareng roulé
root vegetable	racine
rosemary	romarin
rosy/pink	rosé
rue	rue
rum	rhum
rump	culotte

rump steak	rumsteck
runner beans	haricots d'espagne
runny, moist texture	baveuse
rye bread	pain de siegle

S

saddle	selle
saffron	safran
sage	sauge
salad (spring)	salade (de printemps)
salad-green	salade verte
salad-mixed	salade mêlée
salmon	saumon
salmon trout	truite saumonée
salsify/oyster plant	salsifis
salt	sel
salt cod	morue
salt herring	hareng sale
salty	salé
sandpiper	alouette de mer
sardines	sardines
sauerkraut	choucroute
sausages	saucisses/cervelas/mortaderre/andouillette
sautéed	sauté
sautéed in hot frying pan	poëlé
savory	sarriette
scabbard fish	sabre
scallop	peigne
scallops (queen)	coquilles st. jacques (vanneau/banette)
scrambled (eggs)	(oeufs) brouillés
sea bass	loup de mer/bar
sea bream	daurade/pagre commun
seafood	fruits de mer
seafood stew	bisque
sea smelt	abusseau
seasoning	condiment
seaweed/kelp	varèche/aigue
seedless	sans pépins

selection of pork meats	charcuterie
self-service	libre-service
service included	service compris
sesame seeds	graines de sésame
set menu	menu à prix fixe
shad (fish)	alose
shallot	échalote
shandy	panaché
sharp (acidic)	acidulés
shellfish	crustacés/coquillages
shepherd's pie	hachis parmentier
sherry	sherry/xérès
shortcrust pastry	pâte brisée
shoulder	épaule
shredded (vegetable)	émincé
shrimp (brown) (pink)	crevettes (gris) (rosé)
simmered	mijoté
sirloin	faux-filet/aloyau
skate	aigle de mer/raie
skate wings	ailes de raie
slice	tranche
sliced (finely) - meat	émincé
sliver/thin slice	lèche
sloe	prunelle
small	petit(e)
smelt	éperlans
smoked	fumé
smoked haddock	haddock
snacks	casse-croûte
snail (small)	petit gris
snails	escargots/limaçons
snipe	bécassine
snow eggs	oeufs à la neige
soda water	l'eau au siphon
soft	mou
soft boiled	mollet
sole	sole
sorrel	oseille
soup	potage
soup (clear)	consommé
soup spoon	cuiller à soupe

sour	aigre
soused	poché dans un liquide acidulé
soya beans/shoots	pois chinois
sparkling	mousseux/pétillant
spearmint	menthe verte
spicy (hot)	épicé (pimenté)
spider crab	araignée de mer
spinach	épinards
spinach (cooked with)	florentine
spiny lobster	langouste
split peas	pois cassés
sponge finger	boudoir
spoon/spoonful	cuiller/cuillère
spring chicken	poussin
spring lamb	navarin printanier
spring onion	ciboule(tte)
spring roll	rouleau de printemps
spring salad	salade de printemps
squab	pigeonneau
squash	gourde
squeezed	pressé
squid	calmar/encornet
starters	hors d'oeuvre
steak (beef)	steak/steack
steam	vapeur
steamed	cuit à la vapeur
steamed (vegetables)	étuvée/cuit à la vapeur
stew	salmis/ragoût
stewed	à l'etouffée/civet
stewed apple	compote de pommes
stewed fruit	compote
stewing fowl	poule
stock	bouillon
stock (thickened chicken/ meat)	veloutée
straight/neat	sec
strawberries	fraises
strawberry ice cream	glace aux fraises
string (of sausages)	chapelet
string peas	pois mange-tout
strong	fort(e)

stuffed/stuffing	farcies/farce
suckling pig	cochon de lait
sugar	sucre
sugar-light brown	cassonade
sugar peas	mange tout
sultana	raisins de smyrne
sundae ice cream	coupe glacée chantilly
swede	chou navet/rutabaga
sweet	doux/sucré
sweet and sour sauce	sauce aigre - douce
sweetbreads (calf/lamb)	ris (veau/d'agneau)
sweet chestnut	châtaigne
sweet corn	maïs
sweet meats (fruits)	dragées
sweet peppers	poivrons
sweet potato/yam	igname/patate
sweet white wine	i) monbazillac
	ii) sauternes
swiss chard	blette/bette
swordfish	espadon

T

table wine	vin ordinaire
tangerine	mandarine
taramasalata	tarama
tarragon	estragon
tart/pie	tourte
tart (open)	galette
tart (small)	tarte (tartelette)
tart/sour	aigrette
t-bone steak	côte de boeuf
tea	thé
tea-china	thé vert de chine
tea-cup of	une tasse de thé
tea-iced	thé glacé
tea with lemon	thé au citron
tea with milk	thé au lait
tea with cream/lemon	thé au crème/citron

teal	sarcelle
tender	tendre
tenderloin of t-bone steak	tournedos
tenderloin steak (lamb, pork, veal)	médaillon/chateaubriand
thin/lean meat	maigre
thrush	grive
thyme	thym
toast	pain grillé
tomato juice	jus de tomate
tomatoes	tomates
tongue (ox)	langue (de boeuf)
tonic (water)	schweppes
topped/coated with	nappé de
tough	dur
treacle/molasses	mélasse
trifle	diplomate
trifle sponge	boudoir
tripe	tripes
trotters (pork/sheep)	pieds (de porc/de mouton)
trout	truite
truffles	truffes
tuna (tunny)	thon/germon
turbot	turbot
turkey (young/cock)	dinde (dindonneau)
turmeric	curcuma
turnips	navets
two people	pour deux personnes

U

uncooked/raw	cru
underdone (rare)	saignant(e)
urchin	oursin

V

vanilla	vanille
vanilla ice cream	glace à la vanille
veal	veau
veal sweetbreads	ris de veau
vegetables	légumes
vegetables (mixed)	macédoine de legumes
vegetarian dishes	plats végétariens
venison	chevreuil/cerf
vermicelli	cheveux d'ange
vermouth	vermouth
very dry	brut
very rare (cooked meat)	bleu
vinegar	vinaigre
vinegar dressing	vinaigrette
vodka	vodka

W

wafers	oublies/tuiles
waffle	gauffre
walnuts	noix
warm	tiède
water	l'eau
water chestnut	macre
watercress	cresson
water (fizzy)	l'eau gazeuse
water (hot)	l'eau chaude
water ice	sorbet
watermelon	pastèque
water (mineral)	l'eau minérale
water (still)	l'eau non gazeuse
weaver fish	vive
well done (cooked meat)	bien cuit
wheat	froment
whelk	buccin/bulot
whipped	fouetée

whipped cream	i) crème chantilly
	ii) crème fouetée
white	blanc
whitebait	blanchaille
whiting	merlan
wild chicory	barbe-de-capucine
wild mushrooms	champignons sauvages
wild pigeon	palombe
wine	vin
wine (local)	vin du cru
wine (table)	vin ordinaire
wing	ailier
winkle(s)	bigorneau(x)/vignette(s)/vignot(s)
woodcock	bécasse
wood grouse	coq de bruyère
wood pigeon	ramier
wrapped/coated	fichie

Y

yam/sweet potato	patate/igname
yeast cake	baba
yoghurt	yoghourt/yaourt
young turkey	dindonneau
young wildboar	marcassin

Z

zest	zeste
zucchini/courgette	courgette

*For the self-catering tourist
I have included a section of
everyday shopping and
phrases that may prove
useful*

Shops opening:-   usually open at about 9.00 a.m. and closed
for an hour or two for lunch. They remain
open until 5.30 – 7.00 p.m. (6'ish in
Belgium and 6.30 p.m. in Switzerland)

Measurements

100 g – 3.5 oz.	1/2 kg – 1.1 lb.
200 g – 7.0 oz.	1 kg or kilo – 2.2 lbs.

Self-catering and shopping

artificial sweetener	l'édulcorant
bag	sac
bakers	la boulangerie
better	mieux
big	grand
bottle	bouteille
bottle opener	un ouvre-bouteilles
box of chocolates	une boîte de chocolats
butchers	la boucherie
cake shop	la pâtisserie
can you help me?	pourriez - vous m'aider?
cash desk	caisse
cheap	bon marché
cheaper	meilleur marché
chemists	la pharmacie
complaint	une plainte
confectioners	la confiserie
corkscrew	un tire - bouchon
cups	des tasses
cutlery	la coutellerie/des couverts
dairy	la laiterie
delicatessen	la charcuterie/le traiteur
department store	le grand magasin
dining room	salle à manger
do you have…?	avez - vous…?
dozen	une douzaine
enough	assez
expensive	cher
fish monger's	la poissonnerie
flea market	le marché aux puces
frying pan	une poêle
glass	un verre
green grocer's	le primeur
grocery	l'épicerie/le magasin d'alimentation
half kilo	un demi-kilo
half	une moitié
half-dozen	une demi-douzaine
hardware shop	la quincaillerie
health food shop	le magasin de diététique

heavy	lourd
how much?	combien?
hundred grams	cent grammes
I don't understand	je ne comprends pas
I have	j'ai
I like that …	il me plait/je l'aime bien
I want	je voudrais/je désire
I'd like to pay	l'addition, s'il vous plaît
I'll have one of those please	je prendrai un de ceux - là, s'il vous plaît
I'm just looking	je ne fais que regarder
I'm looking for …	je cherche …
ice pack	une cartouche réfrigérante
is there/are there …?	y a-t-il …?
it's …	c'est …
jar of jam	un pot de confiture
kilogram	kilogramme
kitchen	une cuisine
large	grand
larger	plus grand
less	moins
litre milk	un litre de lait
little (a)	un peu
lot (a)	beaucoup
many	beaucoup de
market	le marché
matches	alumettes
may I change this?	pourriez - vous me changer ceci?
may I have a bag please?	puis - je avoir un sac, s'il vous plaît?
may I help myself?	puis - je me servir?
more	plus
much	beaucoup
mugs	des grosses tasses
packet of tea	un paquet de thé
pair	une paire
paper napkins	des serviettes en papier
pastry shop	la pâtisserie
picnic basket	un panier à pique-nique
piece of …	un morceau de …
plastic (made of)	(en) plastique
plastic bag	un sac en plastique
plates	des assiettes

Self-catering and shopping

please give me ...	donnez moi.......s'il vous plaît
please write it down	pourriez - vous l'ecrire, s'il vous plaît?
quarter	un quart
sale	soldes
saucepan	une casserole
scissors (a pair of)	(une paire de) ciseaux
saucers	des soucoupes
shopping area	le quartier commerçant
show me	montrez-moi ...
slice	tranche
small	petit
smaller	plus petit
stainless steel	(en) inox
supermarket	le supermarché
sweets	bonbons
take-away (it's to)	c'est pour emporter
that's all, thank you	ce sera tout, merci
there is/there are ...	il y a ...
third	un tiers
tin/can of peaches	une boîte de pêches
tin-foil	du papier d'aluminium
tin-opener	un ouvre-boîtes
tobacconists	bureau de tabac
too	trop
tube of mustard	un tube de moutarde
tumblers	des gobelets
vegetable store	le primeur
what sort of ...	quelle sorte de ...
where is (the nearest)	où est ....(le/la plus proche?)
wine (white) (red)	vin (blanc) (rouge)
wine merchant	le marchand de vin